Sewing Knits
from
Fit to Finish

Dedication

The future of sewing is in the hands of my daughter's generation.
To Alex, who will help carry the industry forward.

Inspiring | Educating | Creating | Entertaining

Brimming with creative inspiration, how-to projects, and useful information to enrich your everyday life, Quarto Knows is a favorite destination for those pursuing their interests and passions. Visit our site and dig deeper with our books into your area of interest: Quarto Creates, Quarto Cooks, Quarto Homes, Quarto Lives, Quarto Drives, Quarto Explores, Quarto Gifts, or Quarto Kids.

ISBN: 978-1-58923-938-8

Digital edition published in 2018

Library of Congress Cataloging-in-Publication Data

Names: Lee, Linda, 1948- author.

Title: Sewing knits from fit to finish : proven methods for conventional
  machine and serger / Linda Lee.
Description: Beverly, MN : Creative Publishing international, 2018. |
  Includes index.
Identifiers: LCCN 2017043875 | ISBN 9781589239388 (paperback)
Subjects: LCSH: Machine sewing. | Knit goods. | BISAC: CRAFTS & HOBBIES /
  Sewing. | CRAFTS & HOBBIES / Fashion.
Classification: LCC TT715 .L445 2018 | DDC 646.2/044--dc23
LC record available at https://lccn.loc.gov/2017043875

Design, Layout, and illustration: Mattie Wells

Photography: Glenn Scott Photography; except for Lisa Pickel (Blakley), Bliss Studios on pages 10, 11, 43, 45, 46–51, 54, 55, 60–67, 70–75, 77–79, 82, 83, 84 (right column), 85 (top), 86 (top), 87 (top), 88–90, 94–96, 97 (top, middle), 98, 100, 101, 106–110, 111 (bottom) 112, 113 (middle, bottom), 114, 115, 116 (top), 117–119, 121, 122, 123 (top left, top right), 125, 125 (top right, bottom right), 134–136, 138, and 139

Sewing Knits
from
Fit to Finish

Proven Methods for
Conventional Machine
and Serger

Linda
Lee

Creative Publishing
international

Contents

Preface

In the 1980s, I owned a retail fabric store in Topeka, Kansas, called threadWEAR. We specialized in high-fashion fabrics of all kinds. I remember that we usually had only one knit fabric to offer—cotton interlock in just a few colors. That was it! I never saw much in the way of knits to buy, no one asked for them in the store, and I sure didn't sew with them.

Thirty years later, it's a rare day when I don't sew on a knit fabric, my wardrobe is full of knit garments, and the variety of knit fabrics available to the home sewer is enormous. Of course, there is still cotton interlock, but with viscose in all its forms, polyester in prints and solids, and novelty textures and open weaves galore, the world of sewing knits has opened to the garment sewer as no other time in history.

Sewing Knits from Fit to Finish is a comprehensive look at this world of knits. You will learn how to identify the types of knit structures, the different fibers and fiber blends found in modern knits, and the best uses for each of them. How to prepare patterns with good fitting techniques is covered in depth. All of the best sewing and serging techniques for the best seam and hem choices are also included. You will learn how to apply various neck finishes, insert a sleeve, make perfect buttonholes, sew darts, and even how to sew activewear and lingerie.

It's time to sew what you love to wear and make it as professionally as you possibly can. *Sewing Knits from Fit to Finish* will be your go-to resource for tackling the sometimes intimidating prospect of sewing with knit fabrics.

1

Know Your Knits

Other than the singular common characteristic of all knits—
that they stretch—the variety of knits available today is
staggering. Some knits stretch very little, while others
stretch more than you can imagine. From smooth and lus-
trous to loopy and bulky, the range of fibers, textures, and
looks is alluring. Your sewing will be enhanced once you
learn more about the types of knits manufactured today.

Characteristics of Knits

Although the variety of knit fabrics is tremendous, they all share, to some degree, the same characteristics. Knits don't ravel, they generally don't wrinkle, they do tend to shrink, and they all stretch, some a little and some a lot. These characteristics make knit fabrics fun (and usually quick and easy) to sew and very comfortable to wear.

Ravel Resistance

Due to the interlocking construction of knits, they do not ravel. This means that it is not necessary to "finish" the raw edges either inside or outside the garment, which simplifies construction, saves time, and minimizes bulk along the seams and hems.

Many knits look good with simple, smooth, and "unfinished" cut edges. However, novelty knits, such as sweater knits, have ragged edges that are not as attractive, so edge finishing might be necessary on these specialty knits.

Wrinkle Resistance

Most knits are wrinkle resistant, but their particular fiber content and construction technique does determine the degree of wrinkling. Viscose rayon and bamboo knits tend to wrinkle, sometimes badly, while polyester and nylon are nonwrinkling fibers. ITY (interlocking twist yarns) and textural constructions prevent wrinkling, as well.

Shrinkage

Some knits shrink dramatically, others very little. Most knits tend to shrink more than woven fabrics. See page 31 for a way to determine how much your particular fabric will shrink.

A bamboo knit (foreground) and an ITY knit.

Stretch and Recovery

Knits stretch in varying degrees from almost no stretch to 100% beyond their original (prestretched) size, depending on the construction technique, fiber types, addition of elastic fibers (such as spandex), and surface finishes. Recovery, or the way the fabric springs back to its original size after stretching, is important, too. Garments made from knits with good recovery tend not to sag, "bag-out," or lose their shape. Some knits are very stable, with little stretch, and can be sewn just like a woven fabric.

• Stretch Fibers •

Elastic and elastane are the generic terms for a stretch fiber, and spandex and Lycra are the trade names for this fiber. The addition of this fiber aids in the recovery of a knit fabric.

Knits have either two-way stretch or four-way stretch. Two-way stretch knits have elasticity in one direction only. Four-way knits stretch both lengthwise and crosswise.

Many patterns recommend using fabric with a specific degree of stretch. There may be a ruled gauge printed on the pattern envelope or in the catalog so you can measure the amount the fabric stretches to make sure the fabric is appropriate for the garment style.

To determine the degree of stretch, place two pins 4" (10.2 cm) apart along one edge of each direction of stretch. Hold down one end along a ruler and stretch the other end. The amount the fabric stretches is the percentage of stretch. For example, if the 4" (10.2 cm) of fabric between the pins stretches to 5" (12.7 cm), the percentage of stretch is 25%. Check the recovery at the same time. Does the fabric spring back to its original length?

• TIP •

When considering pattern layout, position the pattern pieces on the fabric so the most stretch goes around the body.

Fibers

Knits are manufactured in many fibers that are generally divided into three categories. Each of the fibers can be knitted in almost all weaves and weights.

- **Natural fibers** such as cotton, wool, silk, linen, and rayon are commonly used. These are extremely comfortable because they are soft, absorbent, and breathe well.

- **Organic fibers** such as bamboo, hemp, and soy have similar properties to natural fibers but are grown and manufactured using sustainable and eco-friendly methods.

- **Synthetic or manmade fibers** are easy to care for and hold their shape, but are not absorbent and, therefore, retain heat and may develop static electricity. These fibers include polyester, acetate, triacetate, nylon, and acrylic.

• Rayon: The Semisynthetic Fiber •

Rayon typically falls into the natural fiber category, although it is really a hybrid. Rayon is a generic term for manmade fibers composed of regenerated cellulose derived from trees, cotton, and woody plants.

The first generation of rayon fabric was manufactured in the 1890s under the name "artificial silk" and became commercially available in 1910. The process of producing rayon is called viscose. When referring to fabric, the two terms, rayon and viscose, are interchangeable.

Modal is the second generation of rayon and was developed in 1964 creating rayon that has higher wet strength and is softer than the original. It dyes just like cotton and is long wearing.

Lyocell, the third generation of rayons, was developed in 1990. Tencel® is the trade name. This fiber has excellent cooling properties, is hypoallergenic, and prevents the growth of bacteria, which cause odors.

Rayon and modal are manufactured using toxic solvents that are released into the air. Tencel is manufactured in a more environmentally friendly manner, using solvents that are almost completely recovered.

You may see any of these terms when purchasing rayon fabrics today.

Knit fabics in a variety of fibers. Top row, from left to right: cotton, cotton nylon, rayon. Center row: wool, bamboo, linen. Bottom row: polyester, nylon cotton, acrylic.

Fabrics

Understanding the basic construction of the different knits and their characteristics will help you determine which type of knit works best for any and every pattern choice.

Knits are manufactured in two general groups, weft and warp knits. Weft knits are made from a single yarn looped horizontally to form a row, with each row building on the previous one, just as in hand knitting. Warp knits are made with numerous parallel yarns that are looped vertically at the same time. Most machine-made knits are weft knits. All of these knits are made from four basic stitches, plain, purl, rib, and warp.

• The Four Basic Knit Stitches •

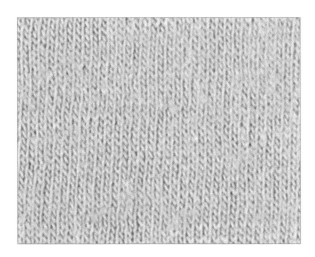

Plain Stitch (Knit Stitch)

The plain stitch is a machine or hand stitch that produces a series of lengthwise ribs on the face and horizontal loops on the back of the fabric.

Purl Stitch

The purl stitch is a machine or hand stitch that produces horizontal loops across both sides of the fabric.

Rib Stitch

The rib stich is a machine or hand stitch characterized by the alternation of prominent ribs on both sides of the fabric.

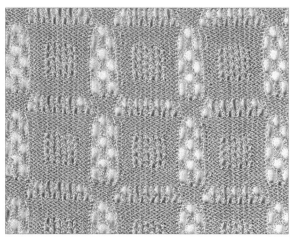

Warp Stitch

The warp stitch is a machine-only stitch formed by looping in a lengthwise direction, forming a zigzag pattern.

Weft Knits

Weft knits are produced using only one yarn with plain, purl, or rib stitches. They include

- Jersey
- Interlock
- Ribbing
- Sweater knits
- Double knits

Jersey

Jersey, a single knit, is the most basic machine-made knit. It has lengthwise ribs (knit stitch) on the right side and horizontal rows (purl stitch) on the reverse.

Jersey is available in just about any variety of fibers and fabric weights, from stable cotton to tissue-sheer silk to super-slinky rayon fabrics, and many include the addition of 2–10% spandex fibers. Jersey's identifying feature is that it curls to the right side when stretched on the cross grain. This makes it somewhat difficult to handle and sew, but it can also be an advantage when you want fashionable raw edges.

Properties:

- Soft and drapeable
- Tends to run easily
- Can be napped, printed, and embroidered
- Ripping out stitches may leave holes and marks
- Substantial wrinkling in certain fibers
- Gathers into fluid folds

Garment Types:

- Tops, tanks, and T-shirts
- Scarves
- Dresses
- Skirts
- Soft jackets and coats
- Pants and leggings

• TIP •

When sewing with jersey, especially tissue and lightweight variations, select pattern styles that are relatively simple without a lot of details such as zippers, plackets, and structured collars.

ITY (Interlock Twist Yarn)

ITY knits are relatively new and are composed of interlocking twist yarns. A twist is added to the yarn to add elasticity.

Properties:

- Very soft, inside and out
- Good drape
- Excellent stretch and recovery
- Wrinkle resistant
- Produced primarily in polyester, often with added spandex

Garment Types:

- Top, tanks, and T-shirts
- Dresses
- Activewear
- Loungewear

Stretch Velour and Velvet

Available in a variety of fibers, stretch velours and velvets have a plush nap on the right side and lengthwise ribs on the reverse.

Properties:

- Plush face has a nap, requiring one-way nap layout
- Fabric should be cut out in a single layer with plush side down
- Fabric layers shift during sewing
- Can be bulky
- Requires special care when pressing
- Nap can flatten, reflecting the light differently and changing color

Garment Types:

- Loungewear, robes
- Tops, T-shirts
- Dresses
- Pants
- Sportswear
- Childrenswear

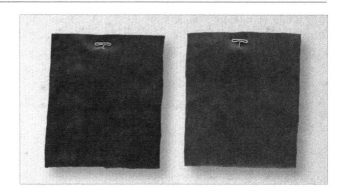

Stretch Terry and French Terry

Stretch terry is distinguished by loops on both sides, like bath towels. French terry has loops on only one side.

Properties:

- Loops can be different sizes, flat, thin, or chunky
- Requires with-nap pattern layout
- Edges shed so edge finishing is required
- Can be bulky
- Edges can curl badly
- Presser foot toes can get caught in the loops
- Tends to snag easily

Garment Types:

- Swim cover-ups
- Loungewear, robes
- Sweatshirts, hoodies, sweatpants
- Casual jackets

• TIP •

The "wrong" or loop side of French terry can be used as the right side for textural contrasts within the same garment.

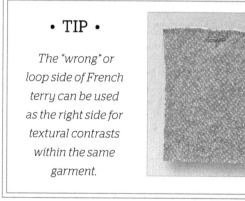

Fleece and Sweatshirt Fleece

Fleece, distinguished by a fuzzy nap on both sides and commonly known as polar fleece, is used in athletic wear for warmth, windproof qualities, and moisture-wicking. Sweatshirt fleece has a smooth side and a fuzzy, napped side.

Properties:

- Cozy hand
- Bulky
- Attracts lint
- Edges curl
- Fuzzy nap side can pill
- Requires with-nap pattern layout

Garment Types:

- Sleepwear
- Tops
- Jackets
- Dresses
- Athletic wear, sweatpants, sweatshirts

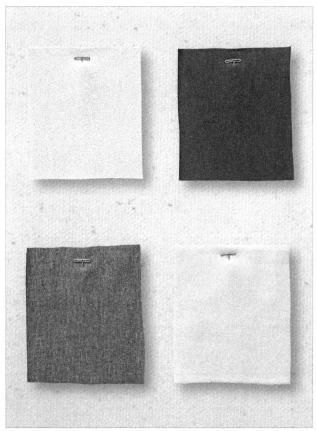

Sweater Knits

Sweater knits feature a wide range of looks, they can be solid or textured with openwork or even intricate stitch patterns, but what sets them apart is that they all resemble hand knitting. Stitch patterns include jacquards, cables, ripples, ribs, and tucks.

Properties:

- Infinite varieties of textures and patterns

- Can distort when stitching and wearing

- Can be bulky

- Can be so open in the weave they are difficult to sew

- May unravel at edges, requiring stabilizing and special sewing techniques

- Requires with-nap pattern layout

Garment Types:

- Scarves

- Jackets

- Tops

- Dresses

Double Knits

Double knits are constructed on a circular machine by interlocking loops with two sets of needles. Both sides look the same. They can be soft or crisp and have very little stretch.

Ponte and Ponte di Roma are two common terms for the new double knits. They are sturdy, often blended with spandex, and are used by top designers to make smooth, sculptural silhouettes.

Properties:

- Stable, firm
- Hold shape well
- Easy to sew
- Edges do not curl
- Good recovery when blended with spandex

Garment Types:

- Jackets
- Tops
- Dresses
- Pants

Interlock

Unlike jersey, interlock fabrics are thicker, with fine ribs on the front and back; both sides look identical. Interlock is a cousin to a double knit but is generally lighter weight and has a bit more drape. It does not have as much recovery as jersey, but it is easier to sew.

Properties:

- Cut edges do not curl
- Firm hand
- Retains shape
- Use with-nap pattern layout
- Puckers and skipped stitches may occur

Garment Types:

- Top, tanks, T-shirts
- Jackets

Rib Knits

Rib knits have prominent ribs on both sides, which gives them the ability to expand and contract more than other knits. They are available in 38–45" (96.5–114 cm)-wide yardage, in a tube, or as narrow rib knit trims. Commonly used for areas that need greater stretch and recovery, such as trims, cuffs, and bands.

Properties:

- Super stretch
- Can distort during stitching

Garment Types:

- Fitted T-shirts, tanks (beefeater shirts)
- Legwarmers
- Hats

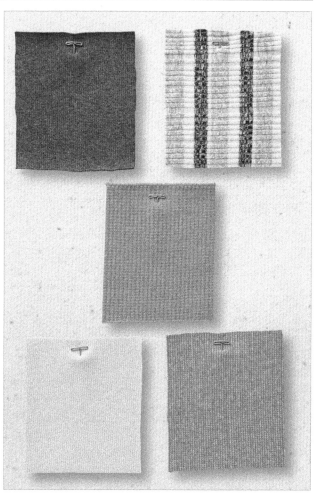

• Slinky Knits •

A variation of a rib knit, this super stretchy knit drapes extremely well, never wrinkles, and is the perfect travel fabric. Acetate and Lycra blends perform exceptionally well.

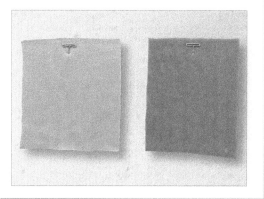

Warp Knits

Warp knits utilize many yarns and feature only one stitch—the warp stitch. Fabric types include tricot, Milanese, and Raschel.

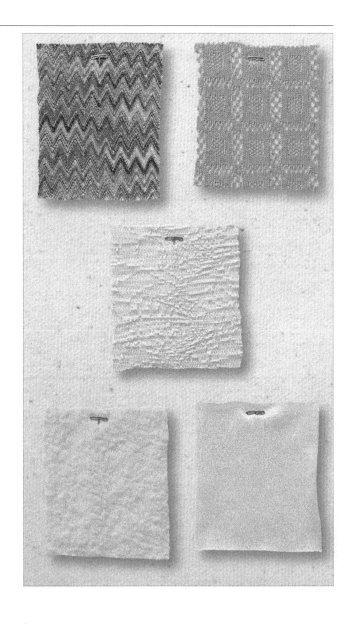

• Milanese and Raschel Knits •

Milanese and Raschel knits are warp knits, but the home sewer rarely sees these terms labeling over-the-counter fabrics. Milanese is smoother and stronger than tricot and is used in more ex-pensive lingerie. Raschel knits are more diverse in their weaves and include lace, tulle, and net-tings, as well as many novelty weaves.

Tricot

This light- to medium-weight fabric is opaque and strong enough to resist runs. Common fibers used are nylon, acetate, and triacetate.

Properties:

- Easy to sew
- Smooth and conforms to the body
- Snags easily

Garment Types:

- Slips, camisoles
- Sleepwear
- Robes
- Linings

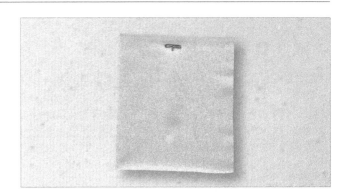

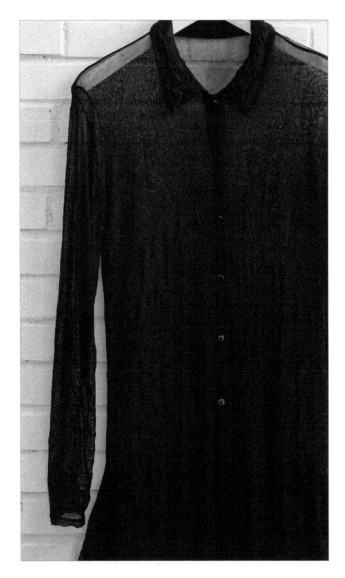

Buying Fabric

In a perfect world, you could shop at your favorite local fabric store and touch every piece of fabric to know which ones feel best for all your projects. If you are lucky enough to be able to buy locally, then shopping with your hands is the most reliable way to find the perfect fabrics.

You will be able to test the stretch and recovery of the fabric, how well it drapes, how soft or crisp it feels, and compare colors in natural light. You will know the degree of rolling at the edges and be able to decide if you want to tackle a knit that rolls excessively. You might even be able to tell if a fabric will pill by folding it with the right sides together and rubbing the layers together, or check to see if it is already pilling on the bolt.

If you can't shop locally, or you are looking for a specific fabric, online buying is the next best option. In this case, though, you need to know the properties and behavior of the different fibers and the technical terms for knit types so you know what you are looking for and can understand the usually brief descriptions. Many of the independent fabric stores and online resources will send you samples upon request.

How Much to Buy

Most knits are between 58" and 63" (1.5 and 1.6 m) wide; the most common width is 60" (1.5 m). Some, but very few, are 45" (1.1 m) wide and these are mostly of Japanese origin. If the fabric is available only in a tube, you can cut along one fold and use it as full-width yardage.

Check the width of the fabric. Compare the width of the fabric to the yardage requirement listed on the pattern envelope and buy accordingly. Or, if you haven't already selected a pattern, but have fallen in love with a fabric, you can estimate how much fabric you'll need using this chart. It is always a good idea to buy at least ¼ yard (22.5 cm) extra to allow for shrinkage and have scraps for technique testing. Here are some guidelines.

Estimated Yardage by Garment/Fit	
T-shirt: Short sleeve	1¼ yd (1.1 m)
T-shirt: Long sleeve	1¾ yd (1.6 m)
Top/Blouse	2½ to 3 yd (2.3 to 2.7 m)
Jacket/Coat	3 to 4 yd (2.7 to 3.7 m)
Dress	2 to 3 yd (1.8 to 2.7 m)
Skirt: Slim	1 yd (.9 m)
Skirt: Full	2 yd (1.8 m)
Pants: Slim	1⅝ yd (1.5 m)
Pants: Full	2¾ yd (2.5 m)

2

Adjusting Patterns for a Better Fit

Perfect fit depends on buying the correct pattern size and then adjusting it for your body. Even when sewing with knit fabrics, simple pattern adjustments will make every garment fit as if it was designed just for you. The following pages explain how to choose the most appropriate fabric, how to measure your body so you can determine your correct pattern size, how wearing ease and design ease play a part in the fit of the garment, and whether you need to make simple fit adjustments to the paper pattern. Basic length and circumference pattern adjustments are also explained in detail.

✂ Fabric & Pattern Selection ✂

It is important to understand the compatibility of your pattern and fabric. You could make the same pattern in five different fabrics and it would probably fit five different ways. Understanding the stretch factor of your knit, the amount of wearing ease that you prefer, and the amount of design ease that is built into the pattern (see Understanding Ease on the opposite page) you will be able to make better fabric and pattern choices and achieve a better fit.

Fabric Selection

Stable knits, such as ponte knit, double knit, and other knits with little or no stretch are not meant to be sewn into styles that are snug or close fitting; instead, they look best made in styles that skim the body. These fabrics need the same amount of ease as patterns designed for woven fabrics. This is considered *positive ease*.

Knits that stretch in all four directions, often used for garments like wrap tops and dresses, athletic wear such as yoga pants, and swimwear, require negative ease in the range of minus ½" to 1" (1.3 to 2.5 cm). *Negative ease* is for garments that are meant to expand to allow the body to move.

Garments made from soft and stretchy knits that stretch in two directions, will probably fit larger than expected, so the amount of ease can be reduced before cutting out the pattern, or you can choose a smaller size pattern. For instance, a fitted or semifitted top made in soft jersey or interlock needs only about ½" to 1" (1.3 to 2.5 cm) additional bust ease.

Pattern Selection

If you are new to sewing knits, select a pattern that is relatively simple, with few fussy details, so that you become accustomed to working with the fabric before having to correct fit issues. Avoid zippers, buttonholes, plackets, cuffs, and tailored details at first.

Conventional Patterns

Conventional patterns are generally designed for woven fabrics that do not stretch. Check the description of the garment and the recommended fabrics on the pattern envelope. If knits are not listed, then you will need to either select a different pattern or measure the pattern to determine how it is designed to fit (see Understanding Ease). If you decide to use a conventional pattern, you might need to start with a smaller or larger pattern size than you typically choose or sew smaller or larger seam allowances.

For-Knits-Only Patterns

Many patterns are designed specifically for knit fabrics and this information appears on the pattern envelope. While a conventional pattern can be made in a knit, it is difficult to reverse that theory. A garment intended for a knit would likely be too small when made in a woven fabric.

Patterns made for knits-only have varying seam allowance widths. The most common seam allowance for conventional patterns is ⅝"-wide, but many patterns for-knits-only have ¼"-wide seam allowances.

• TIP •

Be sure and check your particular pattern and make note of the seam allowance width before you start sewing.

Understanding Ease

Ease is one of the most overlooked aspects of fitting and sewing, but it is one of the most important concepts. There are two types of ease, wearing ease and design ease and, combined, they are used by the pattern designer to create both comfort and style. When determining how a pattern will fit, you will need to consider the amount of ease built into the pattern pieces.

Wearing Ease

Wearing ease is the amount of extra circumference of fabric in a garment that allows you to move and feel comfortable. Wearing ease is a very personal choice. Some people like close-fitting garments, while others prefer a looser fit, even in the same style garment.

Design Ease

Design ease is the amount of extra fabric in a garment that creates the style, as intended by the pattern designer; it is the extra inches (cm) of fabric added beyond wearing ease. If you measure a pattern that would appear to be your size (according to the measurement chart on page 39) and the pattern measurements are much larger than your body measurements, then the designer purposely designed this style to be a loose-fitting garment.

The first words in the pattern description (on the envelope) are indicators of what the designer intended as a fitting category.

- **Fitted.** Garments touch the body without constraint.
- **Semifitted.** Garments skim the contours of the body.
- **Loose Fitting** and **Very Loose Fitting.** Garments hang away from the body in varying amounts.

Design Ease Chart

You can determine how much total ease has been added to a pattern by comparing measurements between the bust, waist, and hip measurements indicated on the size chart to the measurements of the actual pattern pieces (see Measuring Your Pattern for Personalized Fit on page 43). For example, if the size chart indicates a bust measurement of 34" (86 cm) and the pattern measures 38" (96.5 cm), the amount of ease over the bust area is 4" (10 cm). Or, you can refer to the chart on the opposite page for the typical amount of ease added for different garment types and different fitting styles. This information tells you how much ease the garment will have once you finish making it, so that you can make some pattern adjustments, if you wish, for a closer or looser fit.

Design Ease Chart for Woven Fabrics and Stable Knits

The amounts of ease listed in the chart are considered the maximum for knit garments because the degree of stretch of each particular knit fabric determines how much ease you want or need. Use this chart as a baseline for stable knits. For stretch knits, the amount of ease you add is a personal choice based on your shape, how you like garments to fit, and the degree of stretch in the fabric you are working with. Generally, the more the fabric stretches, the less ease you need to add.

> **• TIP •**
>
> *You might want to analyze one of your favorite-fitting garments for comparison purposes. Measure the garment at the bust, waist, and hips and compare those measurements to the same areas on the pattern (see Measuring Your Pattern for Personalized Fit on page 43). This will help you decide if you want to add or subtract ease from the pattern, and where to do so.*

> **• TIP •**
>
> *When fitting people in my workshops, I tend to add about 1 to 2 inches (2.5 to 5 cm) of ease for super stretchy knits, but some people prefer zero or even negative ease.*

Ease Chart for Woven Fabrics and Stable Knits

These amounts are considered the maximum amounts of ease for knit garments.

Style	Bust Ease			Pant and Skirt Ease		
	Blouse/Dress	Jackets	Coats	Full Hip	Waist	Stride Length
Fitted	3" to 4" (7.6 to 10.2 cm)	3½" to 4½" (8.9 to 11.4 cm)	5" to 7" (12.7 to 17.8 cm)	2" to 3" (5 to 7.6 cm)	1" to 2" (2.5 to 5 cm)	1" (2.5 cm) if hips are less than 37" (0.94 m)
Semifitted	4" to 5" (10.2 to 12.7 cm)	4½" to 5½" (11.4 to 14 cm)	7" to 8" (17.8 to 20.3 cm)	3" to 4" (7.6 to 10.2 cm)		1½" (3.8 cm) if hips are 37" to 40" (0.94 m to 1 m)
Loose Fitting	5" to 8" (12.7 to 20.3 cm)	5½" to 10" (14 to 25.4 cm)	8" to 12" (20.3 to 30.5 cm)	4" to 6" (10.2 to 15.2 cm)		
Very Loose Fitting	more than 8" (20.3 cm)	more than 10" (25.4 cm)	more than 12" (30.5 cm)	more than 6" (15.2 cm)		2"+ (5+ cm) if hips are 40" (1 m) or more
	Upper-Arm Ease					
	1" to 2" (2.5 to 5 cm)	2" to 4½" (5 to 11.4 cm)	4" to 5½" (10 to 14 cm)			

Fitted

Semifitted

Loose Fitting

Very Loose Fitting

Garment ease from fitted to very loose fitting.

Taking Accurate Measurements

This section covers the tools you will need, as well as how to take accurate measurements for yourself or for someone else.

Tools

You will need a few specific tools in order to measure yourself (or someone else) accurately.

- **Tape measure.** A tape measure with the number one (1) at both ends, but on opposite sides of the tape.

- **Elastic.** A length of elastic that fits easily around your waist. The width of the elastic should correspond to the width of a waistband, usually 1" (2.5 cm) wide. The elastic is used as a point of reference for taking measurements that begin or end at the waist.

- **Mirror.** A floor-length mirror is very important when taking your own measurements.

- **Measurement Chart.** Photocopy of the chart on the opposite page so you can record your measurements.

Tools for measuring.

Taking Your Measurements

Take all your measurements over the undergarments that you normally wear. Even if you often wear form-fitting bodywear, don't wear it when you are taking your measurements. You want to record realistic numbers.

Measurement Chart

Name: _____ Pattern: _____ Date: _____

Body Area	(A) Body Measurement	(B) Pattern Measurement	(C) Difference between (A) and (B)	(D) Standard Ease	(E) Ease Changes +/–	(F) Amount +/– to Each Seam Allowance	(G) Finished Garment Measurements
Full Bust Circumference							
Shoulder to Bust Point							
Bust Point to Bust Point							
Shoulder Width							
Arm Length							
Upper-Arm Girth							
Back Waist Length							
Waist Circumference							
Full Hip Circumference							
Distance from Full Hip to Waist							
Stride							
Pants Length (From Waist to Floor Minus 1" [2.5 cm])							
Skirt/Dress Coat Length							

The measurements (se opposite page) are the basic measurements needed to determine your starting size and to make preliminary adjustments to your pattern. More fine tuning may be needed once the garment is constructed, but not finished.

Standing in front of the full-length mirror, take the following measurements. For each measurement, make sure the tape measure is level and not pulled too tight. Relax and breathe. Fill in the body measurement (column A) on the measurement chart.

1. Full Bust Circumference: Position the tape measure over the fullest part of the bust and measure around the body. Keep the tape measure level.

2. Shoulder to Bust Point: Measure from the center of the shoulder line to the bust (apex) point.

3. Bust Point to Bust Point: Measure the distance between the bust points.

4. Shoulder Width: Find the point at which the neck bends and the outer point along the shoulder where you can feel the drop-off and measure between these points. If you can't locate either point by yourself, stand in front of a mirror and put a tape measure along your shoulder line and find a distance that is pleasing to the proportions of your body.

5. Arm Length: With the arm slightly bent, measure from the arm drop-off point to just below the wrist bone.

6. Upper-Arm Girth: If you are taking this measurement on your own, attach a small D-ring at the 1" (2.5 cm) mark at one end of the tape measure. Place the tape measure around the upper arm about 1" (2.5 cm) below your armpit. When recording this measurement, add 1" (2.5 cm) to the measurement to adjust for the D-ring attachment.

7. Back Waist Length: Measure from the back of the neck to the waist.

8. Waist Circumference: Wrap and pin the elastic around the waist. Place the tape measure around the elastic and measure, leaving one finger behind the tape measure for a little extra ease.

9. Full Hip Circumference: Find the fullest part of the hips, whether that is high or low, and measure at that level.

10. Distance from Waist to Full Hip: Measure the distance from the elastic around the waist to the full hip.

11. Stride: Place one end of the tape measure right under the elastic at the back waist, bringing it through the crotch to the bottom of the elastic in the front. Add 1" (2.5 cm) to this measurement for sizes below 16 and add 2" (5 cm) to this measurement for sizes above 16.

12. Pants Length: Without shoes, stand on the 1" (2.5 cm) mark at one end of the tape measure. Bring the tape up to the bottom of the elastic along the outside of the leg.

Skirt/Dress/Coat Length: The easiest way to determine a skirt, dress, or coat length is to measure the finished length of a garment that you enjoy wearing. You can also do this to determine pants length.

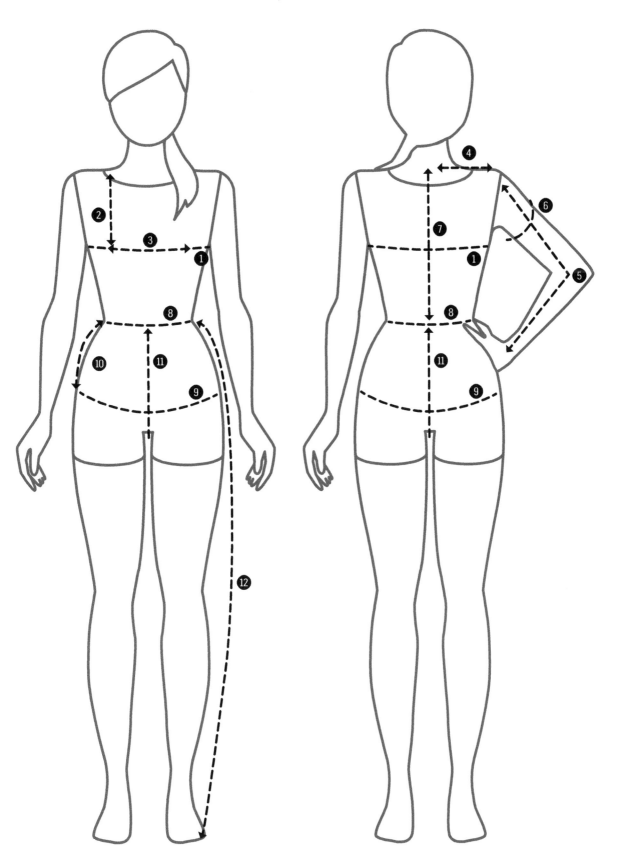

Buying a Pattern

Choosing the best pattern size for a top, jacket, and some dresses is based on your bust measurement. The size for skirts, shorts, pants, and close-fitting dresses is based on your hip measurement. For a full-skirt you can use your waist measurement as a guide.

Look at the size chart on the pattern envelope and find the size closest to your body measurement. This will be your starting size. Once you know your pattern starting size, you can purchase the pattern and then make adjustments for a more personal fit.

Standard Pattern Size Measurements									
	XS	SM		MED		LG		XL	XXL
SIZE	6	8	10	12	14	16	18	20	22
Bust	31" 77.5 cm	32½" 81.3 cm	34" 85 cm	36" 90 cm	38" 95 cm	40" 100 cm	42" 105 cm	44" 110 cm	46" 115 cm
Waist	24½" 61.3 cm	25½" 63.8 cm	26½" 66.3 cm	27½" 68.8 cm	29" 72.5 cm	31" 77.5 cm	33" 82.5 cm	35" 87.5 cm	37" 92.5 cm
Hip	34" 85 cm	35" 87.5 cm	36" 90 cm	37" 92.5 cm	39½" 98.8 cm	41½" 103.8 cm	43½" 108.8 cm	45½" 113.8 cm	47½" 118.8 cm

Measuring Your Pattern for a Personalized Fit

Actually measuring the tissue pattern (called flat pattern measuring) and comparing these measurements to your body, keeping ease allowances in mind, is the most important aspect of fitting.

Many commercial patterns feature several sizes in one envelope, all marked on the same tissue (multi-sized patterns). This is quite handy if you are one size on top and a different size through your hips.

If you are using a multisized pattern with lots of cutting lines, use a red pencil to mark your starting size at the corners of all the pattern pieces directly on the tissue.

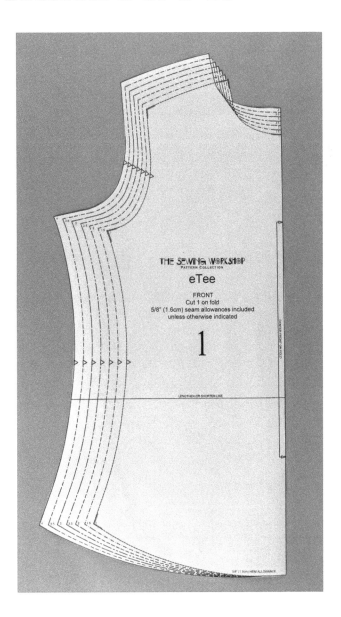

• Regarding Seam Allowance •

When measuring your pattern, remember that you are determining "finished" measurements, so do not include seam allowances. Check the pattern to confirm if the seam allowance is ⅝" or ¼" (15 or 6.4 mm) wide.

Make a template that marks the seam allowance width. Use the template to mark the seam allowances at the points you are measuring, in order to record finished measurements.

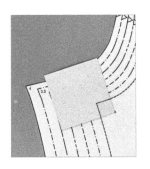

Tools

Gather these tools to measure your pattern accurately.

- Tape measure
- Red pencil: A pencil by Prismacolor, Carmine Red 200045 has an eraser and is perfect for pattern work.
- Calculator
- Measurement chart (see page 39)

How to Measure the Pattern

Measure the pattern pieces as indicated and fill in the pattern measurement (column B) in the measurement chart. Remember, most patterns include seam allowances, so do not include them in your pattern measuring; measure between fold lines and center front lines to get finished measurements.

Additionally, most patterns are either one half of the total garment and are cut as two pieces or they are cut on the fabric fold (resulting in a total piece). Add the dimensions of the front and back pieces to get total circumference.

Upper-Body Measurements

Locate the bust point: Many patterns use this symbol to indicate the bust point.

Back waist length: Measure from the back of the neck to the waist.

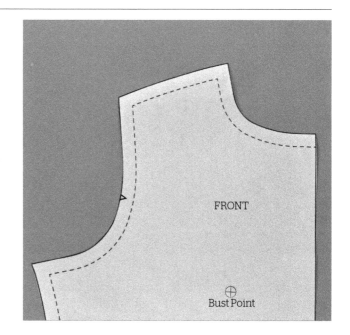

FRONT

⊕
Bust Point

• How to Determine Bust Point If There Is No Symbol •

To check that the bust indicator placement is correct for your body or to determine your bust point if there is no indicator, use a ruler to draw a slightly diagonal line from the center of the shoulder line toward the apex of the bust that is equal in length to the "shoulder to bust point measurement." Draw a second and horizontal line from the center front to intersect with the first line (A); this line should equal in length half the "bust point to bust point measurement." The intersection of these two lines is your bust point.

Full bust circumference: Measure the pattern front and back and add the two measurements. If the pattern front and back are cut on the fold, you will need to multiply the measurement by two for a full body circumference.

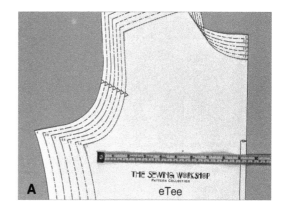

THE SEWING WORKSHOP
PATTERN COLLECTION
eTee

A

Shoulder width: Measure the shoulder from the neck to the top of the sleeve.

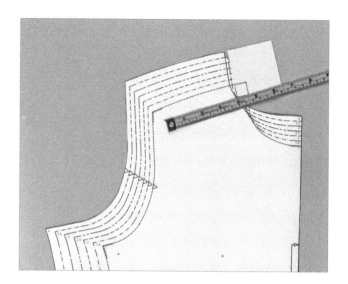

Arm girth: Measure the pattern just below the shaped sleeve cap.

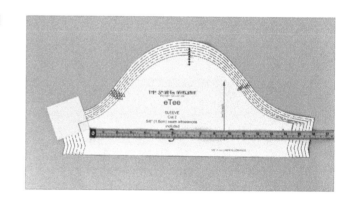

Lower-Body Measurements

Waist circumference: There may be a waistline indicator on your pattern. If so, use it to measure the waist circumference. If there is not an indicator, refer to your "back waist length" measurement. Or, you can hold the tissue pattern up to your body and mark where the pattern hits your waist on the pattern. Measure from seam allowance to seam allowance at the waist marking on both the front and back patterns. Add these measurements and multiply the number by two if the front and back pieces will be cut on the fabric fold.

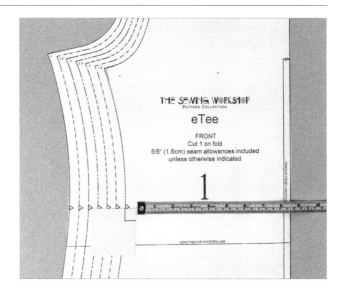

Full hip circumference: Refer to your "distance from waist to full hip" measurement and measure that distance on your pattern from the waist down toward the hem, and make a pencil mark. Then measure the hip circumference at that pencil mark as for the waist above.

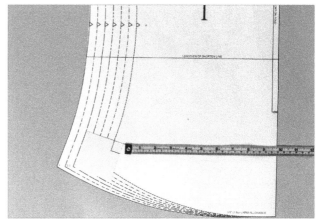

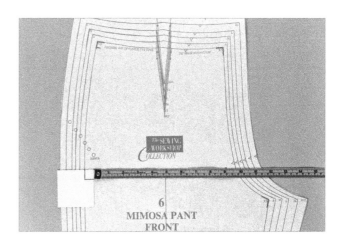

Stride: With the tape measure on its edge (not flat), measure the front and back crotch from the waist seam to the inseam and add the two measurements for the total stride length.

Skirt length: Measure from the waist seam to the finished hemline along the side seam.

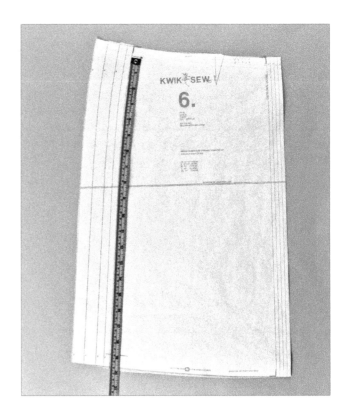

Pants length: Measure from the waist seam to the desired finished hemline along the side seam.

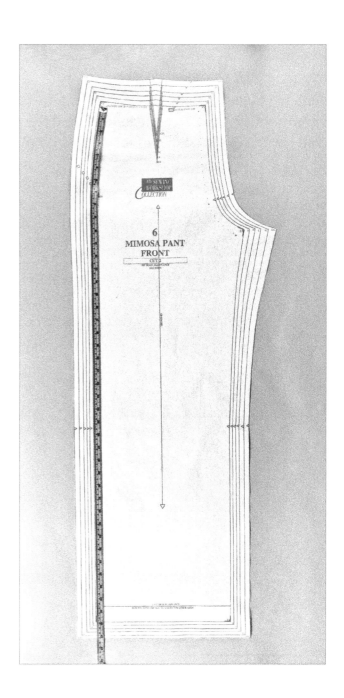

Tissue Fitting

Actually trying on the paper pattern is a quick way to determine how well a knit garment will fit. You will be able to immediately see if the pattern is too small. This works best for a top pattern and is more difficult for a pants pattern.

Cut out the pattern slightly outside your starting size cutting lines. Pin any darts or other details that shape the pattern. Then, pin the pattern together at the shoulder and side seams with the seam allowances on the outside.

Stand in front of a mirror and take a look. Since you will usually be working with one half of the pattern, make sure that the center front and center back are aligned with the center of your body. You will know instantly whether the pattern is too small or too large and whether it sits well on your shoulders.

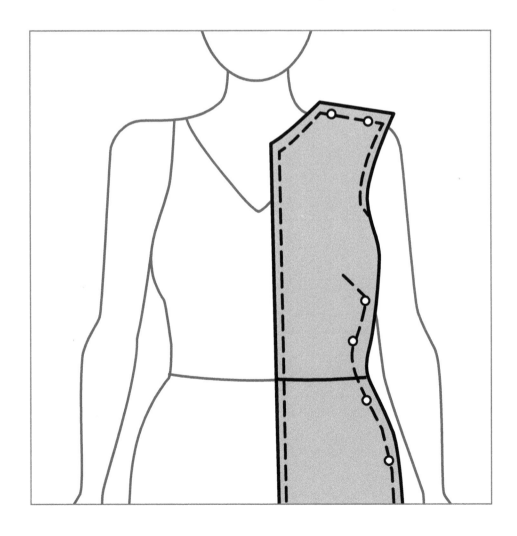

• TIP •

If you are having trouble getting the tissue to sit properly at the armhole, place small sections of tape along the seamlines of the armhole. Then clip to the seamline (to the edge of the tape) to allow the seam to open and the tissue to sit better on your body.

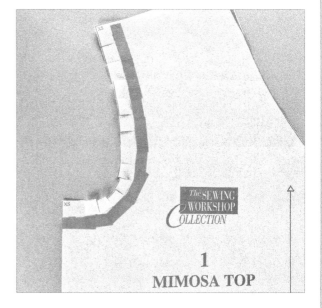

Check fit in these areas in the following order:

For a top:
- ✔ Waist length
- ✔ Bust location
- ✔ Total length
- ✔ Shoulder width
- ✔ Bust circumference
- ✔ Waist and hip circumference

For a bottom:
- ✔ Stride length
- ✔ Total length
- ✔ Hip circumference
- ✔ Waist circumference

You may have to remove the pin-fitted tissue after every checkpoint, make an alteration, and then pin the tissues back together and try on again in order to check each area.

Adjusting Your Pattern

Making adjustments to your pattern before cutting out your fabric eliminates potential fitting problems and improves the overall appearance of the finished garment.

Tools

Having the right tools will help you measure and adjust patterns more professionally. Here are the essentials.

Pattern drafting paper

Use paper that is see-through, stays together with clear tape, and shows hand-drawn lines well.

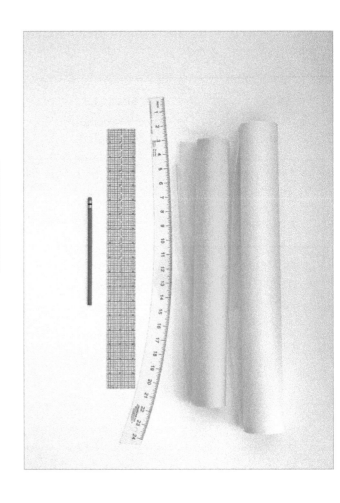

> **• TIP •**
>
> *Medical exam paper or architectural canary tracing paper works well.*

Red pencil

Use a pencil rather than a permanent marker because you may want to make changes and need to be able to erase all markings.

Removable tape

Scotch Removable Tape can be moved and/or removed without damaging the tissue pattern when you need to fold and unfold the tissue or add paper to extend the existing pattern paper.

Rulers

Rulers used for drafting patterns are available in either metal or plastic. Clear plastic rulers are easier to use and may be less expensive. You'll need a variety of styles.

Straight ruler

Use a flexible clear ruler that is not too large and has ⅛" (3 mm) grid marks.

Hip curve

This is the most universal of the large curved drafting tools.

French curve (not shown)

This is a classic drafting tool with several curves for restoring and smoothing shaped seamlines.

Considering Ease

You have already noted your body measurements (column A) and the pattern measurements (column B) on the measurement chart, so now you need to compare the two figures and record the difference in column C.

Then refer to the ease chart on page 37 and record the standard ease for your pattern style in column D. Consider how the amount of designer-added ease (column D) relates to the actual amount of ease (column C) and based on how you want the garment to fit, compute the amount of change that needs to be made to the pattern and enter it in column E.

Then divide that amount of change indicated in column E by the number of seams affected by the desired change. The total amount to be added or subtracted to a circumference is divided by the number of seams in the garment and this amount is entered in column F. For example, if there are only side seams, the amount to be added or subtracted is divided by 4 (because there are 4 cut edges/2 seams). If there are side seams and center front and back seams, the amount is divided by 8 (8 cut edges/4 seams).

Length Adjustments

Make all length adjustments, no matter whether to a top or a bottom first, before any circumference adjustments. If there are length adjustment lines indicated on the pattern, use them. If not, there are specific places to make these adjustments (see below).

Basic Lengthening Technique

1. Cut the pattern apart along the adjustment line.

2. Tape a piece of pattern paper to one cut edge of the original pattern. Use the red pencil to extend the grainline (which may be a center front or center back foldline) (A).

3. Measure and mark the desired amount you want to lengthen the pattern on the grainline you just drew.

4. Draw a line perpendicular to the grainline. Tape the remaining pattern piece along this new line.

5. Use a straight or curved ruler to restore the cutting lines (B).

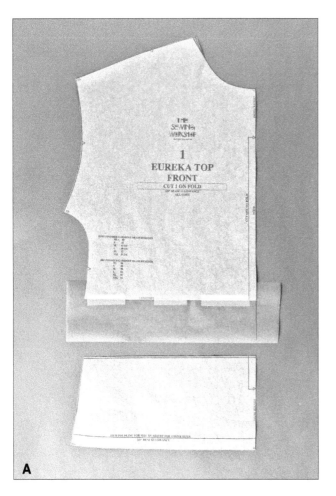

A

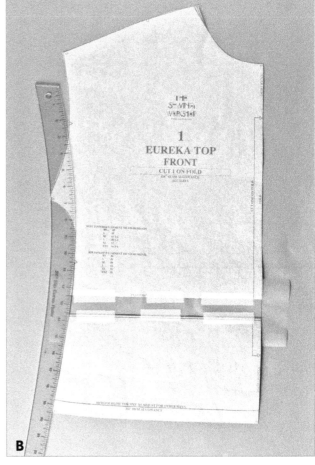

B

Basic Shortening Technique

1. Fold the pattern on the adjustment line, one half the desired amount that you want to shorten the pattern. Make sure the straight grainlines meet. For example: To shorten a pattern 2" (5 cm), make a 1" (2.5 cm) fold.

2. Use a straight or curved ruler to restore the cutting lines (A).

Where to Lengthen and Shorten

If there are no length adjustment lines marked on the pattern pieces, use the following guidelines.

Lengthen or Shorten Tops, Jackets and Some Dresses at the Waist

Locate your waist (use your back waist measurement) on the pattern and measure up about 1" (2.5 cm) and make a mark. Draw a line at the mark perpendicular to the straight grainline. Lengthen or shorten the back and front pattern pieces along this line, making sure the new lengths match at the side seams. Restore the cutting lines.

Lengthen or Shorten Sleeves

Draw a line perpendicular to the straight grainline approximately 2" (5 cm) down from the bottom of the sleeve cap and lengthen or shorten along the line. Restore the cutting lines.

Lengthen or Shorten Pants

Fold the leg pattern in half so the finished hemline aligns with the top of the inseam. Draw a line perpendicular to the straight grainline and lengthen or shorten along this line. Restore the cutting lines.

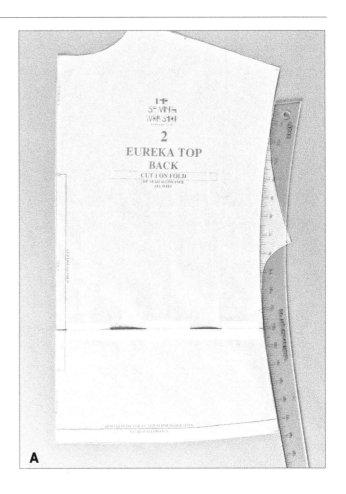

A

Lengthen or Shorten Skirts

Most skirts can be lengthened or shortened at the bottom edge unless there are design details that prevent this, such as pleats, godets, or flared sections. If there are design details, find an area on both the front and back pattern pieces that is the straightest and without design details and draw a line perpendicular to the straight grainline. Lengthen or shorten the front and back pieces along this line. Make sure the adjustments are the same to the front and back patterns. Restore the cutting lines.

Circumference Adjustments

After making all length adjustments, alter a pattern's width in the following order. Find the columns noted on the Measurement Chart on page 39.

Shoulder Width

1. On drafting paper, trace in red the original cutting line of the front and back armhole.

2. Referring to column C, mark the desired width change along the shoulder cutting line, at the corner of the shoulder and armhole, either inside (to narrow) or outside (to widen). Do not include seam allowances.

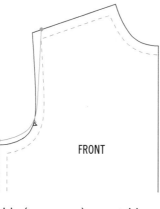

FRONT

3. Place the tissue pattern on top of the traced front armhole, with the new shoulder marking on the pattern over the original tracing. Pivot the pattern until the bottom of the original armhole is in line with the side seam cutting line. The distance inside or outside of the original starting size will be the same as the amount of shift at the side seam. Trace the original armhole in its new position onto the pattern. Repeat on the back pattern piece.

Waist and Hips Width

1. **For long T-shirts or tops without a waistline seam,** mark the waistline and add or subtract width along it at the side seam cutting lines of both the front and back patterns using column F as your guide.

2. If there are center front and center back seams, you might want to distribute the amount of width change between all the seams. Refer to page 31.

3. Use a hip curve to redraw the new cutting lines.

4. If the pattern has a seam at the waistline, draw a diagonal line from the waist up to the underarm point of the front. Cut along the line from the waist up to, but not through, the underarm cutting line. Spread or overlap the pattern by one fourth the total amount needed. Repeat on the pattern back.

1. **For pants or skirts**, refer to column F and mark the desired width change at the waistline and at the hipline on the side seam cutting lines of both the front and back pattern pieces. If there are center front and center back seams, you might want to distribute the amount of width change between all the seams. Refer to page 31.

2. At the side seams, use a hip curve to blend new cutting lines from hip to waist. Use a straight edge to redraw center front and back seams.

Arm Width

1. Draw a vertical line through the center of the sleeve. Draw a horizontal line perpendicular to the vertical line along the cap line.

2. Cut on these lines up to, but not through, the outer edges, forming a hinge.

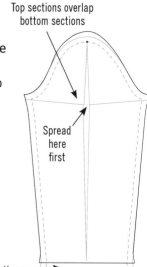

Top sections overlap bottom sections

Spread here first

Adjust to original length →

3. Place drafting paper under the cut lines. To enlarge the width, pull the cut edges gently apart the desired amount and tape in place. To reduce the width, move the cut edges of the upper sections so they overlap those of the lower sections, forming a diamond shape in the center of the sleeve. Tape in place. Adjust or restore cutting lines, as needed, to the original or desired length.

Bust Fullness

There are two methods for adding ease in the bust area without adding darts. You can only make these adjustments if the pattern indicates a bust point or you locate yours on the pattern (page 45).

To Add Minor Ease

1. Draw a horizontal line from the side seam to the center front through the bust point. Cut along this line and spread the sections an even ½" (13 mm).

2. Mark a point ¼" to ¾" (6.4 to 19 mm) from the side seam at the spread area. Use a French curve to draw a curved shape at the side seam.

3. When sewing the garment together, ease the back to the front in the bust area to make the seam match from top to bottom.

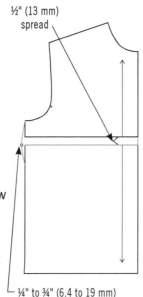

½" (13 mm) spread

¼" to ¾" (6.4 to 19 mm)

To Add Major Ease

1. Locate and mark your bust point. Starting midway between the shoulder seam and the armhole notch, draw a line perpendicular to the straight grainline.

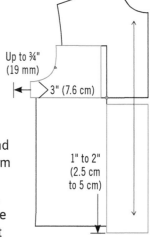

Up to ¾" (19 mm)

3" (7.6 cm)

1" to 2" (2.5 cm to 5 cm)

2. Pivot this line and extend it vertically to the bottom of the pattern. At 3" (7.6 cm) below the armhole, draw a line from the side seam to the center front perpendicular to the straight grainline.

3. Cut through all lines. Move the armhole section out (up to as much as ¾" [19 mm]) for a total of 1½" (3.8 cm) ease across the complete front bust area.

4. Move the lower center front section down 1" to 2" (2.5 to 5 cm) depending on your bust size and the amount that similar garments ride up.

5. Use a hip curve to restore the side seam and bottom hem, a French curve to restore the armholes, and a straight edge to align the center front.

To add additional bust ease, refer to standard methods of adding a bust dart recommended for woven fabrics.

3

Getting Ready to Sew

It takes more than just tossing the fabric on a table to cut out your pattern. Early care in preparing your fabric and good cutting and marking practices go a long way toward making your final garment look better.

8
MixIt
TOP SLEEVE
CUT 2
5/8" SEAM ALLOWANCE
ALL SIZES

The SEWING WORKSHOP
COLLECTION

HEM FOLDLINE
3/4" HEM ALLOWANCE

Equipment

The number one piece of equipment you need to sew knits is a sewing machine. While any project can be sewn with this singular piece of equipment, there is no question that adding a serger to your equipment ups the quality and makes sewing faster, especially if you are interested in borrowing design details and good finishing techniques from ready-to-wear knit pieces. A variety of pressing tools is also essential, starting with a good iron.

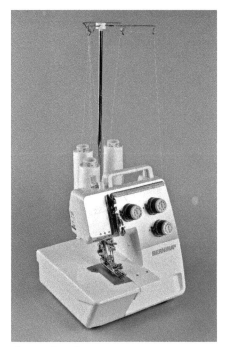

Cover Stitch

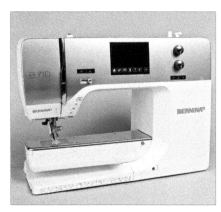

Sewing Machine

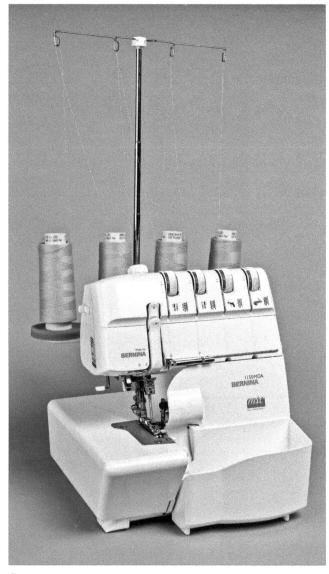

Serger

Sewing and Serging Equipment

The range of sewing machines, from the most basic to the highly sophisticated is almost endless. But the reality is that all you need is a sewing machine that is in good working order with a quality straight stitch and a zigzag stitch. Also helpful is a good selection of presser feet, like a walking foot. A model that has a built-in even-feed feature is also useful.

Presser Feet

The most common challenge when sewing knits is that the fabric doesn't feed through the machine easily. It may hang up and create stitches that are too small or the fabric my get lodged and jammed in the throat plate.

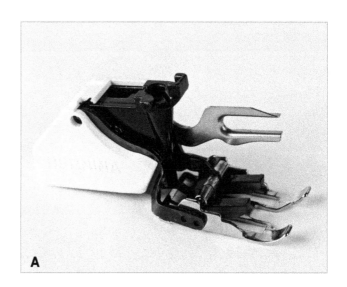

A sewing machine is designed with a presser foot that rests on top of the fabric putting some pressure on the fabric, and with a set of feed dogs under the fabric that feeds the fabric through the machine. With knits, the feed dogs carry the under layer of fabric through just fine, but the top layer often gets left behind and the fabric doesn't feed evenly. The easy solution to this problem is to either attach a walking foot or engage the even-feed feature (if your machine has it). These help the machine feed both layers of fabric through the machine at the same time.

A

The walking foot (sometimes called an even-feed foot) is an extra accessory (A) and usually is not included in the price of the machine. It is not an inexpensive addition and it is absolutely essential for sewing any type of knit, in any weight. Built-in even-feed features are usually available in the higher-priced sewing machine models.

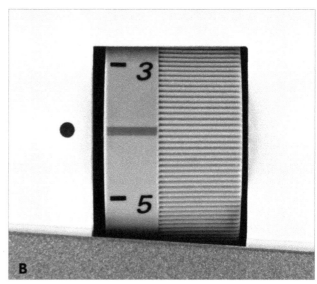

If you do not have a walking foot or one is not available for your sewing machine model, try decreasing the presser foot pressure. This usually involves turning a knob (B) or engaging an icon on a screen. By decreasing the pressure of the presser foot on the fabric, the fabric may feed through more evenly.

B

Needles

The best needle choices for sewing knits are either universal or jersey needles in sizes 75" (11 mm) or 80" (12 mm). Heavier knits require larger needles. A 70" (10 mm) needle might be used on a tissue weight, while a thick and heavy sweater knit may require a 90" (14 mm) needle.

For super stretchy knits or when an elastic fiber such as spandex has been added to a knit, a stretch needle in the appropriate size might help eliminate skipped stitches.

It is important to have a variety of needle types and sizes on hand when making test samples to determine the best needle for sewing every type of knit fabric.

Caution: Ballpoint needles can leave holes in the knit, even after laundering the garment.

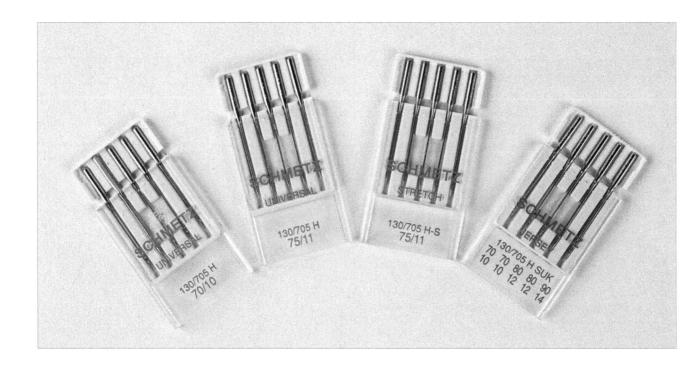

Throat Plates

There are a variety of throat plates available for most sewing machines. Newer models that are capable of machine embroidery, feature a throat plate with a 9 mm (⅓ inch)-wide needle opening in order to make multimotion and decorative stitches, but this wider opening ca n cause knits to jam. Throat plates with smaller-sized openings are more suitable and useful in preventing the fabric from jamming into the opening. A single-hole throat plate is the very best, but can only accommodate straight stitching. The 5 mm (.20 inch)-wide throat plate is the best compromise, allowing you to straight and zigzag stitch and sew buttonholes while moving the fabric through the machine easily.

• TIP •

When optional throat plates are not available, a couple of layers of clear tape placed over the opening in the throat plate may do the trick.

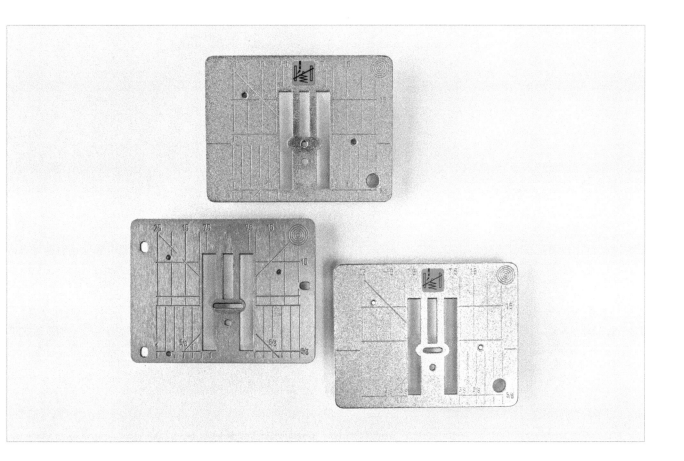

Serger

A serger is a machine that produces the multithread interlocking stitch commonly used in ready-to-wear for both seam construction and edge finishing knits. A combination of needles and loopers carry and interlock the threads to produce fully finished wrapped edges.

When purchasing a serger, make sure that the machine produces two-thread, three-thread, and four-thread stitch formations. You might want to test stitch on even the thinnest of knits before buying it. The finished stitch should be flat without rolling or torque, with even stitches on the face and underside of the fabric, and a floating thread along the very edge of the fabric.

Other features to look for include a large range of stitch length and width adjustments and a setting called a differential feed (A). Differential feed changes how the fabric is fed through the machine and allows the fabric to remain flat without puckers, waves, or drawing up.

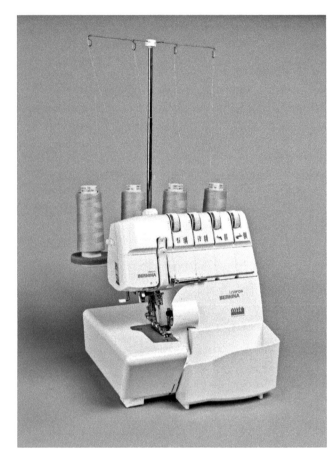

A

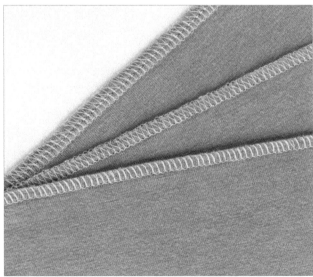

Coverstitch Machine

For years, the home sewer was unable to duplicate the double-needle-looking stitch that is universally used in ready-to-wear. But now, thanks to the coverstitch machine, duplicating ready-to-wear is possible.

The most popular coverstitch is produced with two needles and three threads. There are two rows of straight stitches on the top and a series of looping stitches on the bottom. It is most commonly used for hemming, with the connecting stitches on the bottom side covering the raw hem edge, producing a beautifully finished hem on both sides. There is often the option to use three-needles for three parallel rows of straight stitches, as well as a variety of width choices.

The coverstitch is available as a feature on some sergers (usually higher-priced models) or as a dedicated machine that looks like a serger but only produces coverstitches.

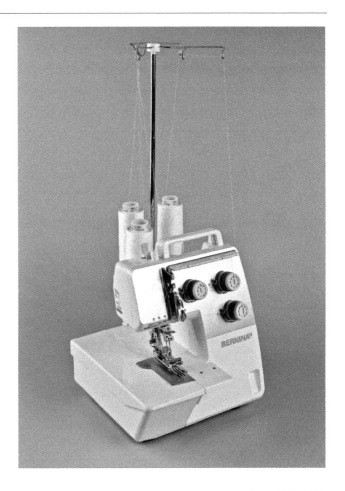

Pressing Equipment

Pressing tools help you press specific areas correctly, building shape into a garment. As long as you have a good-quality steam iron and a sturdy ironing board, you can add various pressing tools as the need arises.

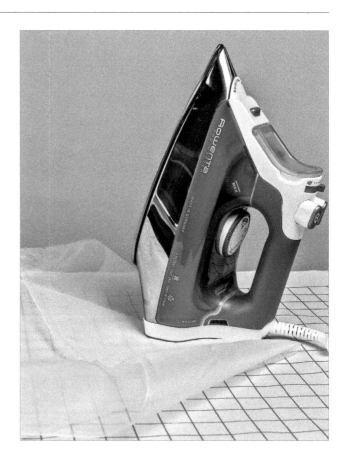

Iron

Buy the best iron you can afford. Choose an iron that produces good steam, has a smooth sole plate, and doesn't spit or leak.

Ironing Board Cover

An ironing surface needs to breathe to achieve a good press. A cotton canvas cover is the best choice, and a printed grid allows you to align hems and edges.

Press Cloth

Use a press cloth to help prevent melting and scorching and reduce potential shine. To make a press cloth, use pinking shears to cut an 18" x 18" (46 x 46 cm) piece of silk organza. This sheer cloth allows you to see what you are pressing and it reduces shine.

Tailor's Ham and Holder

Press darts, neck bindings, and curved areas, including seams over a tailor's ham. Not only does this tool help retain the shape of a garment, but it raises the area to be pressed and prevents creasing other areas.

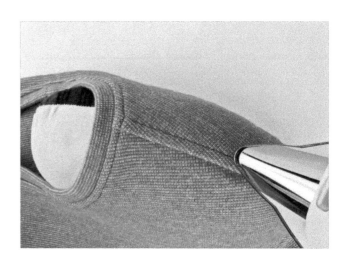

Sleeve Board

A sleeve board (below) allows you to press narrow tubular areas such as pant legs, sleeves, and cuffs easily.

Tailoring Board

This unique pressing tool (right) is made of hard wood and has many different shapes and edges to help refine your pressing. The wood absorbs the steam, leaving a crisp press. It is especially useful when pressing seams open on straight edges and curves, especially in small areas. It also doubles as a ham holder.

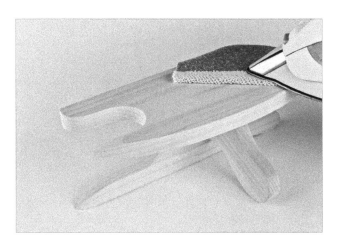

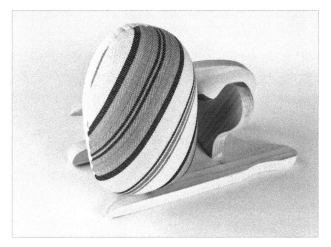

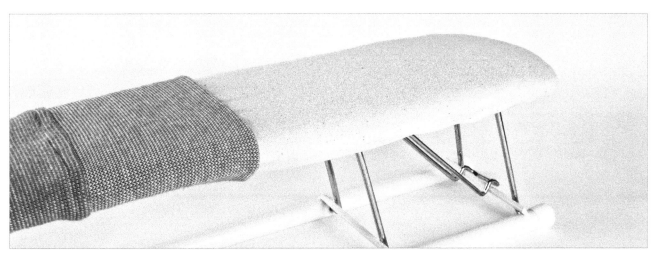

Prepping the Fabric

Almost all knit fabrics are washable. Some shrink and change character more than others, so testing a sample is important.

Testing and Pre-shrinking

Cut a 4-inch (10 cm) square of the fabric and throw it in the washing machine along with other laundry and wash it in hot water and dry it, too. Then measure the laundered square to see how much it changed. Some knits will shrink in both directions, others in one direction only. This will help you determine if you need to preshrink the entire fabric yardage before cutting out the pattern and best way to launder the finished garment.

Washing knit yardage usually results in some distortion of the grain. Off-grain knits can rarely be straightened, so you will need to decide if perfect grain (a stripe, perhaps) is essential.

You may decide to preshrink the fabric using the hottest settings, but treat the finished garment differently. You might want to wash the finished garment in milder settings or even hand wash

and air-dry it. This helps the fabric wear better and last longer.

Dry cleaning is always an option for any knit. One particular fabric, wool-jersey might benefit from dry cleaning. If you want to keep the original look and feel of wool jersey, then it definitely should be dry cleaned. Washing it will shrink and felt it, turning it into a completely different fabric.

Straightening Grain

Establishing the straight of grain of a fabric is one of the most important things you can do you insure that your garment hangs nicely, but it can be really difficult to determine the straight of grain of a knit.

Try to find the vertical ribs on the right side of a knit and use a chalk marker to mark a few rib lines throughout the yardage. Try to align these marks parallel to the edge of the cutting surface for regular references when you are laying out the pattern pieces.

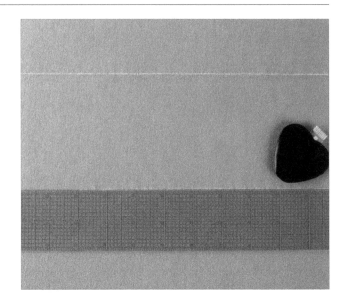

Pressing

As with all sewing, careful pressing techniques are essential. Knits are a bit unique.

Always test press your knit fabric to determine the best temperature and to make sure that the fabric doesn't melt, pucker, or scorch. Some knits press well, while others hardly retain a crease. Whatever the situation, over pressing can result in unwanted shine. Knit garments should have a softly pressed finish. Use an up-and-down motion, as opposed to a back-and-forth motion to avoid distorting and stretching the fabric. Don't overpress.

Rather than waiting to press the garment once it is finished, press as you sew.

Laying Out the Fabric

Most knits do not lie flat. More than likely, the selvages draw the fabric up at the edges. Use a rotary cutter to remove the selvages. There may be a texture difference between the selvage and the fabric or some small holes running parallel to the selvage that can be your guide for trimming (see below).

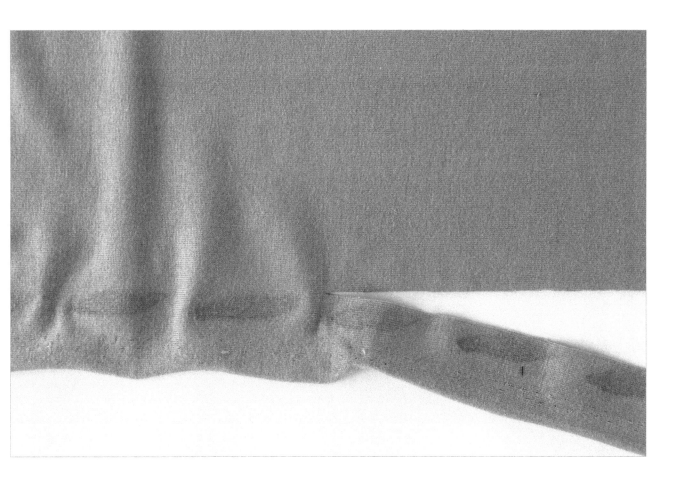

Knits are best cut out in a single layer of fabric. If you are unsure whether you have enough fabric, use pattern drafting paper to trace pattern pieces that need to be cut more than once and to complete half-pattern pieces such as the back of a T-shirt pattern that is cut on the fabric fold. Laying out as many pieces as possible all at once also prevents moving the fabric too much and minimizes shifting. This is also very helpful when working with stripes or plaids that need to match at the seams.

Work on as large a surface as possible, preferably on a cutting mat (so you can use a rotary cutter). Don't let the ends of the fabric fall off of the table. Roll the fabric up at one end if needed. Make sure that the pattern pieces are arranged on the fabric with the most stretch going around the body.

Many knits have a nap that can't be see when the fabric is flat on the table. Lay out all pattern pieces in the same direction so there are no shade differences that might appear when the garment is finished.

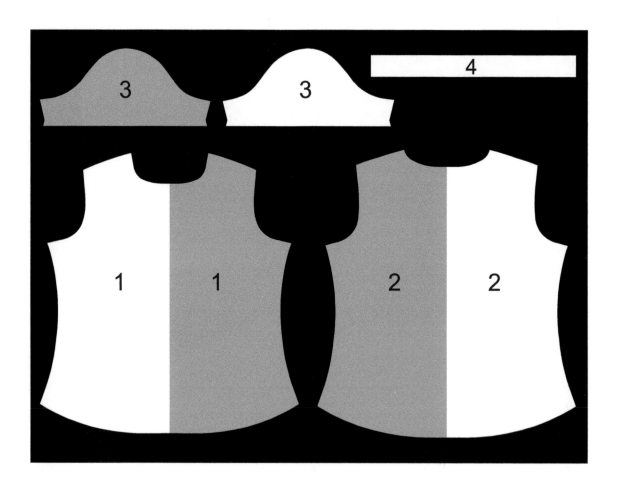

Pinning and Cutting

Although you can use pins to secure the pattern pieces to the fabric, fabric weights hold the pattern pieces and fabric in place while pins tend to shift the fabric, making cutting less accurate.

Since many knits do not ravel and, therefore, may not be finished on the edges, you want as smooth a cut as possible; a rotary cutter is the best option for cutting even edges. If you prefer shears, use the largest blades that you can handle for a smoother cut.

When there are straight edges on the pattern pieces, use a see-through ruler, together with a rotary cutter, for smooth cuts.

To hold fabric layers together during sewing, glass head silk pins are my pins of choice. Look for pins with a really sharp point that slip through the fabric smoothly. Don't sew over pins, throw bent and dull pins away, and replace your pins frequently.

Because pins don't typically work well on such fabrics as lace, crochet, and other open weave novelty knits and thick sweater knits, use small clips to hold the edges together while sewing.

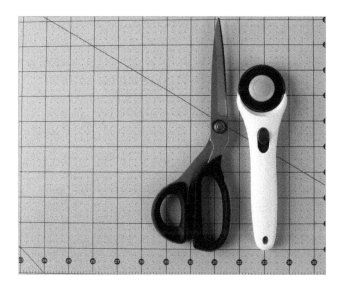

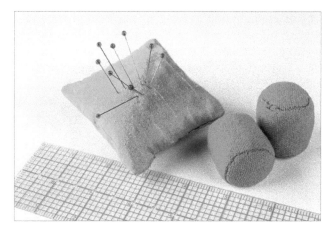

Marking

It is essential to mark all notches, circles, and other important match points before the cut piece is removed from the cutting table. It is almost impossible to re-establish the perfect match of pattern and fabric.

Fabric marking pens and pencils claim to "disappear" with either water or air. Test these tools on a scrap of fabric first to make sure they live up to their packaging. Chalk markers disappear as you are working with the fabric. Tailor's tacks and small snips into the seam allowance are the best marking methods for knits.

Interior Markings

The most dependable and accurate method of marking knits is with tailor's tacks. These are used primarily for interior markings such as circles, squares, and triangles, which are used to mark seamlines, darts, tucks, and buttonhole and button placements.

To Make Tailor's Tacks:

1. Mark the location for a tailor's tack by inserting a pin through the mark on the pattern and into the fabric (A).

2. Pull the tissue away from the fabric. Using a fine hand-sewing needle and a single strand of thread, take one stitch where the pin enters the fabric, leaving a 1" (2.5 cm) thread tail (B). Then take one more loose stitch. Cut the thread to leave another 1" (2.5 cm) thread tail (C).

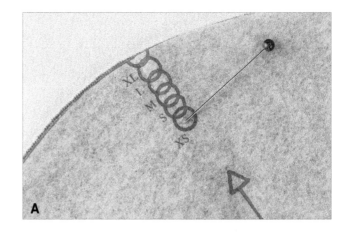

A

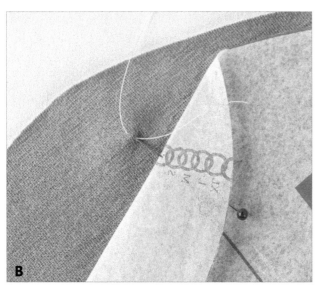

B

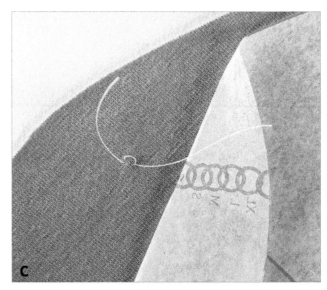

C

Exterior Markings

When there are notches along the outer edges of the pattern, use small trimming scissors to snip into the seam allowances. Cutting around notches that extend outward from the cutting line lifts the fabric too much and distorts the cutting line.

Marking Open-Weave Knits

For open-weave knits such as stretch lace, crochet, or other novelty textures, use small safety pins to mark interior markings and outer notches.

Interfacing

By choosing to work with a knit fabric because of its stretch factor, it seems logical that an interfacing should be able to move and stretch along with the fabric. The decision to interface a knit is all about the style of the garment and the type of knit. Lightweight knits may need to be supported with interfacing. Many stable knits such as ponte do not need to be interfaced at all.

The usual locations that might benefit from interfacing are no different from those of woven fabrics. Facings, plackets, collars, cuffs, and buttonholes are areas that may need to be supported.

Tricot interfacing is the most common choice, and the more lightweight, the better. Whether you use a fusible or a sew-in interfacing is a personal choice, but fusible interfacings have improved so dramatically that there is no reason not to consider using them.

All interfacings should be tested on a scrap of fabric before committing to the actual project to make sure they don't change the hand feel of the fabric.

The interfacing can actually be preshrunk on the fabric itself before permanently fusing it in place. With the garment wrong side up, position the interfacing in the desired location. Hold the iron over the work and without touching the fabric or interfacing, activate the steam. Once the interfacing has drawn up, press it firmly to fuse it to the fabric.

When interfacing a small, curved pattern piece such as a collar, it is easier to interface a section of fabric, and then cut out the pattern from the preinterfaced yardage. When laying out the pattern pieces on the yardage, identify where you will be positioning these smaller pieces and chalk-mark the area. After the major pieces have been cut, you can interface these smaller sections of fabric.

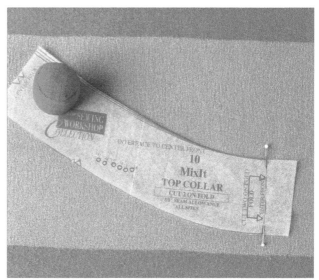

Testing Stitches

Eliminate potential sewing issues by test sewing on scraps of your actual fabric. Experiment with different needles, threads, presser feet, and sewing aids such as paper stabilizers and throat plates with smaller stitch openings, before ever starting the actual project. This testing actually saves time in the end.

Thread

For a sewing machine:

Good-quality, cross-wound polyester thread is the best choice. The thread comes off cross-wound spools evenly, adding to the quality of the stitches. Polyester thread has more strength than cotton and stitches are not as apt to pop during normal wear and tear.

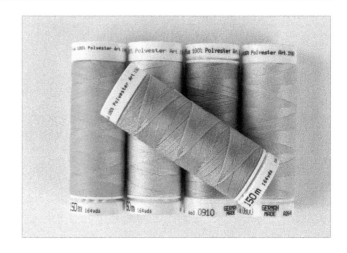

For a serger:

Buy four spools of regular sewing thread to match your fabric. Use one in your sewing machine and three in the serger needle(s). This method insures the best match through the project.

Buy large cones of good quality polyester thread made specifically for serging to use in the loopers. Don't be tempted to buy large, inexpensive cones, these tend to be slightly heavier with thick and thin sections and they produce lots of lint. The most refined, smooth threads for serging are also threads designed for machine embroidery.

For a softer, more blended serged edge, use matching color woolly nylon in the lower looper.

Stitch Quality

When making test samples, use the same fabric you will be using in your project and under the same set of conditions. For example, test on a single layer, a double layer, and an interfaced layer. Practice stitching in multiple directions until you get the right combination of needle, thread, stitch length, and stitch width.

Problems that need to be sorted out and solved are skipped stitches, puckering, too much stretching, minimal fabric feeding, and throat plate jams. Every knit fabric behaves differently, so there are no hard-and-fast rules. It takes some experimenting to find the right combination. Making test samples will help eliminate these problems.

• A Tissue Paper Fix •

Even after finding the right combination of needle, thread, and stitch type, you might want to try another easy fix. Position a scrap of pattern tissue paper under the work and on top of the throat plate. Stitch through both the fabric and paper. The tissue paper adds stability to the stitch and it is easy to tear away once the work is free from the sewing machine.

4

Seams and Hems

It is best to determine what kind of seams and hems are most appropriate for your type of knit and your particular project before you start tackling the construction of your garment. Experiment with both your sewing machine and your serger.

Types of Seams

There are so many ways to seam knit fabrics and because knits don't ravel, you won't even need to clean finish the raw edges. You can use your sewing machine, your serger, or a combination of both machines.

Sewing Machine Seams

There are four basic sewing machine seams suitable for knits: straight stitch, double-stitched, zigzag stitch, and programmed knit stitch.

- **Straight stitch seam.** This is the simplest of all of the seam options. Stitch a line of straight stitches along the seamline. Press the seam open. Use this seam for garments that are semifitted or loose-fitting, garments that don't have a lot of strain on the seams.

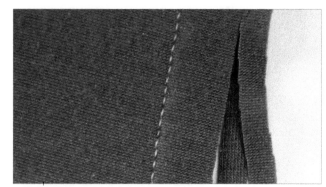

- **Double-stitched seam.** Stitch a line of straight stitches along the seamline. Stitch a second row of stitching ¼" (6.4 mm) from the first line, in the seam allowance, and trim close to this line of stitching. Use this seam when the edges are curling and preventing the seam from staying flat.

- **Zigzag stitch seam.** Start with a machine zigzag setting of 0.5 mm (.02 inch) wide by 2.5 mm (.10 inch) long. The settings may vary with the weight and type of fabric. Use this seam for garments that are close fitting and need to stretch during wearing.

- **Programmed knit stitch.** This stitch is similar to the zigzag stitch, but the length and width are automatically set in the sewing machine software. Some distortion might occur because it is sometimes difficult to make machine adjustments. Use this stitch for garments that need to stretch during wearing. It is a difficult stitch to rip out so make sure it is your final stitch.

Samples of four sewing machine seam finishes (from top): Straight stitch with seam pressed open, double-stitched, zigzag stitch, and programmed knit stitch.

Overlapping Seams

This specialized seam type is used on thick knits whose edges look good when left raw. Fabrics such as felted wool and wool-blend bouclé are the perfect fabrics to sew with overlapping seams in order to reduce bulk.

1. To sew an overlapping seam, first cut away the seam allowance from the edge of one of the garment pieces (the edge that will overlap). Use fabric chalk to mark a line indicating the seam allowance on the corresponding garment edge. Place a strip of double-faced craft tape within the remaining seam allowance, then remove the paper to expose the adhesive (A).

2. Place the trimmed edge over the taped edge, matching the raw edge to the chalk line, and finger-press it in place. Edgestitch along the raw edge. Remove the tape and stitch ¼" (6.4 mm) from the first stitching (B).

3. Trim the excess seam allowance on the wrong side of the seam (C).

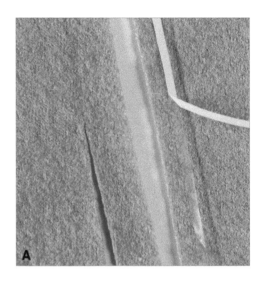

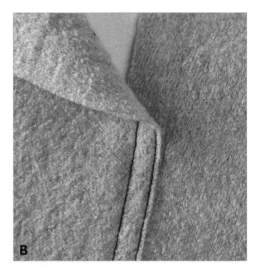

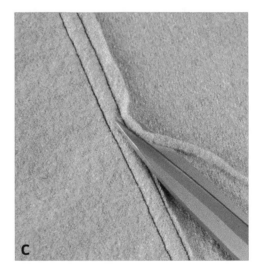

Finished jacket with overlapping seams.

Combination Seam

If you prefer to clean finish raw edges for a more polished look, the simplest option is to first sew a seam using any of the standard sewing machine seams. Then finish the raw edges together with a three-thread serger stitch.

This seam and seam finish can be used on any type of garment, including tops, pants, jackets, and dresses. It tends to be most appropriate for midweight knits or knits that don't ravel but don't really look very good with edges left raw, such as novelty and sweater knits.

Serged Seams

Serging is often referred to as overlocking because a serger actually produces an overlocking stitch. All sergers are different, but most can sew a two-, three-, or four-thread stitch. Some sergers can even sew a five-thread stitch (three-thread overlock stitch with a two-thread chain stitch). The most common serger stitches used on knits are three- and four-thread stitches.

Three-Thread Stitch

The finer three-thread stitch uses threads in one needle, the upper looper, and the lower looper. It is the perfect choice for seams on tissue-weight knits, airy laces, and open weave knits in fairly loose-fitting garments. Otherwise, it is used as the raw edge finish in the combination seam for all other types of knits.

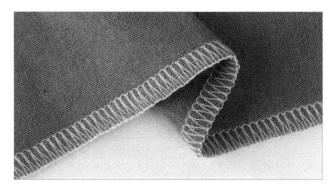

Four-Thread Stitch

The four-thread stitch combines threads in two needles, the upper looper, and the lower looper. With the additional needle thread, the stitch is more hard wearing than the three-thread stitch and can be used to stitch construction seams and is rarely used in combination seams. As a sturdy stitch, it is often the choice for athletic wear, children's clothes, and garments such as T-shirts that are close fitting and are worn and laundered often.

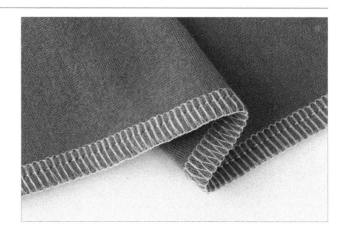

• How to Remove Serger Stitches •

Work from the front and use the tip of a seam ripper to cut the needle thread(s) near one end of the serging. Continue to cut this thread about every 2" (5 cm) (A).

Pull out each section of loose needle threads with tweezers. It might be easier to pull the thread at the center of each cut section (B).

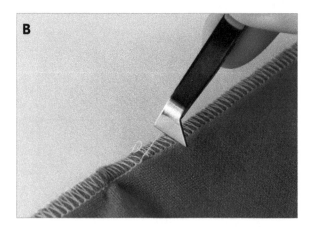

Pull the looped thread away from the edge in one continuous motion (C).

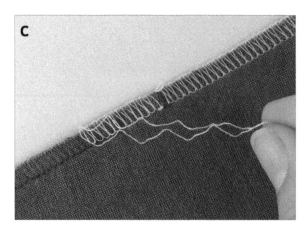

Flatlocked Seams

A flatlocked seam is a reversible serged seam that features loops on one side and ladder stitches on the other. The edges of the seam are butted together rather than overlapped. A two-thread flatlock is particularly suitable for use on stretch lace and other open-weave fabrics that are too bulky to sew conventionally because the ladder stitches blend into the weave of the fabric and are almost invisible. It is not a suitable seam for fabrics that ravel.

Not every serger is capable of flatlocking because it is done with only two threads (one needle and lower looper) so the upper looper needs to be blocked or deactivated. Refer to your owner's manual.

To stitch a two-thread flatlock, use the left needle and set the lower looper tension to 5.0 or looser. Use a 2.5 mm (.10 inch) stitch length, a 3.5mm (.14 inch) stitch width, and set the differential feed between 1.5 and 2 mm (.06 and .08 inch).

Engage the cutting knife to cut off the seam allowances as you stitch. Once you have stitched the seam, remove the garment from the machine and turn the work to the right side, gently spread the seam until it is flat. This allows the loose stitches to form a ladder on the right side of the fabric connecting the two seam edges.

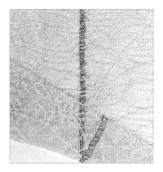
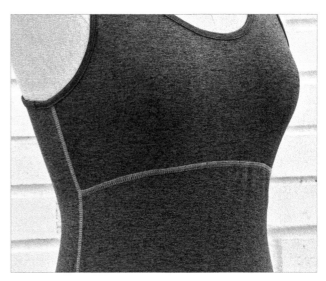

Stabilizing Seams

Certain areas of a garment may need to be stabilized to prevent them from stretching out when the garment is hanging or being worn. Areas that usually need attention are necklines, shoulder seams, and waistlines.

The easiest way to stabilize these areas is to use narrow strips of fusible tricot. You can either cut ½"- (13 mm)-wide strips from yardage or purchase it precut. Since tricot is a knit and has some give, the stabilized areas are controlled to some degree while allowing some natural movement of the garment.

When a garment requires stabilizer, center the strip over the seamline on the wrong side of the fabric. Fuse the strip in place. Then sew the seam, catching the tricot in the stitching. At the shoulder seams, a strip is needed only on the back piece.

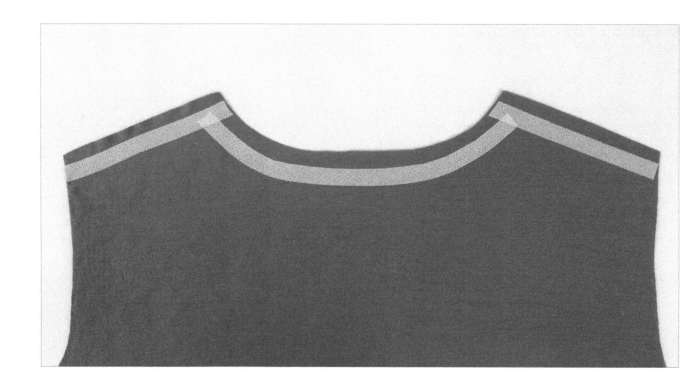

Types of Hems

Hemming a knit garment is almost always the last step, so it's very important to select the right type of hem for your knit and to execute it well.

Unturned Hems

Leaving a hem unfinished used to be a sign of poor quality, but many high-end designers are utilizing the nonravel advantage of knits as planned finishes in designing knit garments. You can leave the cut edge as it is or serge it.

A serged edge is generally a hidden finish, but a carefully stitched line of serging is a perfectly acceptable finished hem choice. A serged edge adds polish without adding bulk and eliminates the challenges of machine stitching a hem on a knit garment.

Turned Hems

Most hems are turned to the wrong side in some fashion and may be finished or unfinished on the wrong side of the garment.

• Techniques for Perfectly Even Hems •

No matter how the hem is ultimately finished, these techniques insure perfectly even hems every time. They should be done right after the garment has been cut out and before any construction begins.

Pressing Template

1. Determine the desired finished width of the hem allowance, and cut a strip of tag board the desired width by 12" (30.5 cm). A manila file folder does the trick.

2. While the garment pieces are still flat, place the template on the wrong side of the hem. Bring the hem allowance up and over the template, matching the raw edge of the fabric to the top of the template. Press through all layers (A).

3. This establishes a memory crease for when it's time to hem the garment.

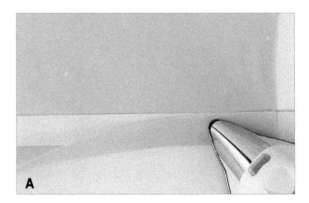

Fusible Web Tape

1. Apply strips of fusible web tape on the wrong side of the hem near the edge. Leave the paper covering in place during the normal construction of the garment.

2. Once you are ready to hem the garment, remove the paper covering, turn the hem to the wrong side, and press the hem with an iron to fuse it in place (A).

3. Once the hem is fused in place, stitching is easy. The hem will stay in place without shifting, stretching, or puckering during stitching (B, top).

Single-Fold Hems

Use one of the two techniques for marking perfectly even hems or simply measure and pin a hem in place. Once the hem is folded one time to the wrong side, it is ready to stitch. Here are five stitch choices:

Straight Stitch (sewing machine)

A straight stitch (A) is simplest and most invisible. Leave the edge raw or finish it with a three-thread overlock stitch formation. This hem is used on garments that are semifitted to loose fitting. Straight stitches on fitted garments can pop open when the garment is stretched.

Zigzag Stitch (sewing machine)

A small zigzag stitch (B) allows the fabric to stretch without popping stitches. Experiment with length and width settings; a good place to start is with a 2.5 mm (.10 inch) length and 1.5 mm (.06 inch) width setting. This is a good stitch to use when making a fitted garment.

A

> • TIP •
>
> *If the hem buckles using a zigzag stitch, try placing extra pattern tissue paper between the throat plate and the fabric (see page 79).*

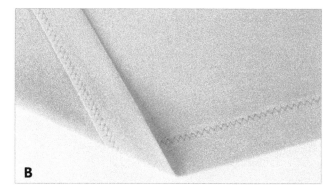

B

Double Needle Stitch (sewing machine)

A sewing machine double needle has two needles on a single shaft, so it requires two upper-thread sources and one bobbin thread. Double needles feature a variety of widths between the two needles, from 2 mm to 4 mm (.08 to .16 inch). This type of needle produces two rows of straight stitches on the right side of the fabric and a series of connecting zig-zag-type stitches on the wrong side. This stitch does resemble a common ready-to-wear hem, except it does not cover the raw edge on the inside hem edge and the stitches don't stay flat, they tend to produce a tunnel between the row of stitches (C).

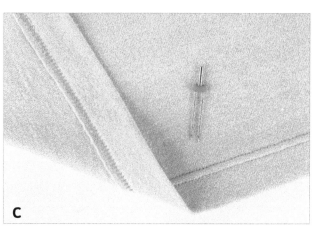

C

Coverstitch (coverstitch machine)

A coverstitch looks like a double needle stitch with two rows of straight stitches on top and connecting stitches on the bottom, but this stitch is flatter, covers the raw edge of the hem and looks the most professional of all of the hem stitch options.

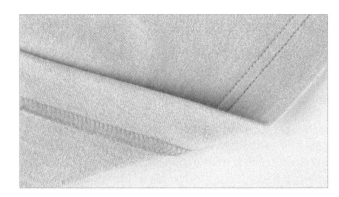

Blindstitch (serger)

A blindstitch produces a smooth hem, invisible from the right side of the garment. It requires a special blindhem presser foot (A), which can be adjusted to barely catch the outer fabric, while overlocking and finishing the inner raw edge at the same time (B).

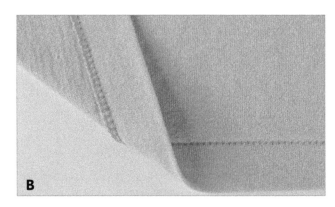

Double-Fold Hems

Occasionally, lightweight sweater knits and other novelty textured knits don't have smooth and attractive looking raw edges. These knits tend to look better with double fold hems. You'll want to test a double fold hem on a fabric scrap to make sure it is not too bulky.

1. Stitch the same distance from the edge as the width of the final hem. Press the hem to the wrong side using the stitching as a pressing guide (A).

2. Move the needle position to the right. Turn the hem a second time, the same distance as in step one, and don't press it. This is a turn-as-you-go hem, so start stitching along the inner folded edge, turning the hem as you stitch. Leave the needle down as you reposition and turn the hem as you advance the stitching to complete the hem (B).

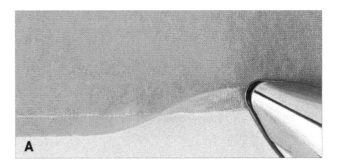

Designer Hems

In addition to raw edges and traditional turned hems, the racks are full of knit garments that feature creative edgings.

Selvage Hems

Many knits have novelty selvages, perhaps ruffled or woven with a contrasting thread (A). This is particularly true on lacey and other open and textured knits. There are a few hem techniques that showcase these novelty edges.

One option is to incorporate a selvage in the design of the garment, planning its placement and using it as a substitute vertical or horizontal hem depending on the direction of the stretch (see opposite).

Another option is to cut away the selvage and then reattach it in another location.

When planning to use a selvage in another place, cut off the selvage, leaving some additional fabric width to work with later. In most circumstances, a selvage can be added back using flatlocking (B). See page 89 for flatlocking instructions.

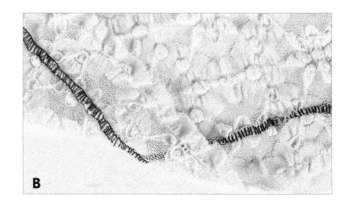

Lettuce-Edge Hems

Lettuce edges are wavy edges that can be sewn on a sewing machine or a serger. Refer to your machine manual for the specifications. They are particularly suitable for jersey, a fabric that naturally curls to the right side on the crossgrain when it is stretched.

Set your machine for a wide enough zigzag stitch to cover the curly edge of the fabric; pull the fabric as you sew. When you pull the fabric as you sew, it curls, and the zigzag covers the curly edge. As with all decorative treatments, experimenting with settings is essential.

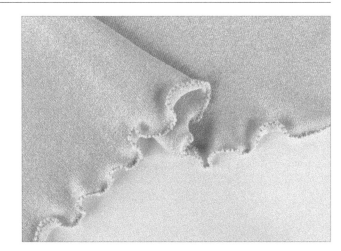

Lettuce edges made on a sewing machine (top) and a serger (right).

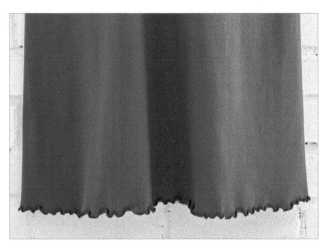

A finished garment with a lettuce-edge hem.

Bound-Edge Hem

When sewing heavy fabrics such as sweater knits, the fabric may be too thick to turn and stitch, so binding the edge is a great solution. The binding material should be a nonbulky knit.

1. Determine the desired finished width of the binding. Cut the binding knit on the crossgrain four times the desired finished width by the length of the edge, plus a few inches (cm). You might have to join several widths of the binding to obtain the necessary length.

2. With right sides together, stitch the binding to the edge of the garment and then stitch the narrow ends of the binding at the point at which they meet (A). Trim away excess binding.

3. Fold the binding over the raw edges, pin, and then stitch in the ditch, catching the binding fabric on the wrong side (B).

4. Trim the excess fabric near the stitching on the wrong side (C).

5

Basic Construction Techniques

Constructing a knit garment is similar to making a woven garment, with some processes being exactly the same and others quite different. A major difference is in the handling the fabric. Since the fabric does not ravel and edges may not need to be finished, there is less work. Working with knits requires a more delicate touch in order to get refined results.

Order of Construction

Constructing a garment in a particular order allows you to access various areas of the garments more easily and finishes the details perfectly.

Below is the standard order of construction for tops and pants.

Tops

1. Hem prep
2. Darts/tucks/zipper (if applicable)
3. Shoulder seams
4. Neck/collar finishing
5. Side seams
6. Sleeves/armhole finishing
7. Complete hems

Pants

1. Hem prep
2. Darts/tucks/zipper (if applicable)
3. Side seams
4. Inner leg seams
5. Crotch seam
6. Waist finish
7. Complete hem

Neck Finishes

There are many ways to finish a neck opening on a knit top; however, a fabric binding is the most common. Neck bindings are perhaps the most visible components of knit garments, so they need to be handled with care.

Binding

Binding, the popular ready-to-wear technique for finishing a neck opening, is an easy method for the home sewer to duplicate.

Cutting the Binding

If a binding pattern piece is included with your pattern, then use it. If there is no pattern available, then use the following formula to make your own binding.

Measure the *finished* circumference of the neck opening on the seamline of the paper pattern pieces; do not include shoulder and other seam allowances.

To calculate the length of the binding, determine ⅞ths of the original circumference (divide the circumference by 8 and multiply that number by 7 or multiply by .875). The binding should be shorter than the original circumference.

To calculate the width of the binding, decide how wide you want the visible amount of the binding to be. Multiply that number by 2 and add the width of two seam allowances.

For example:

½" (1.25 cm) visible width × 2 = 1" (2.5 cm) + 5/8" seam allowance (3.2 cm) × 2 = 2¼" (5.7 cm) cutting width

Every knit differs in its stretch factor, so this calculation is only a starting point. If a knit is extremely stretchy, the binding should probably be cut shorter. If the knit is fairly stable, it might need to be longer. You will need to apply the binding and then try on the garment and see how easily it slips over your head, and evaluate how it fits and shapes the garment neckline. You might need to remove the binding, cut a new and shorter binding, and try again.

Preparing the Binding

1. Fold the binding in half lengthwise with wrong sides together and press. If the edges curl and prevent you from pressing the binding flat, use a narrow strip of fusible web tape to fuse the layers together (A).

2. With right sides together, stitch the narrow ends of the binding together to form a circle (B).

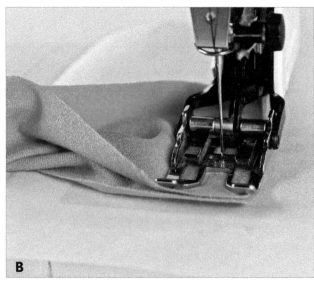

3. In order to apply the binding evenly around the neck opening, divide both the binding and the neck opening into quarters. Start by folding the binding in half with the seam at one end. Clip into the seam allowance (but not through the seamline) at the opposite end fold (C).

4. Refold the binding, stacking the seam on top of the clip mark to find the quarter markings. Clip into the seam allowance at these two new end folds (D).

5. To quarter-mark the neck opening, pinch the shoulder seams together and clip into the seam allowance of the front and back at the folds (E).

6. Then, pinch the front and back clips together and clip into the seam allowance to mark the end folds. These clips will not necessarily be located at the shoulder seams (F).

C

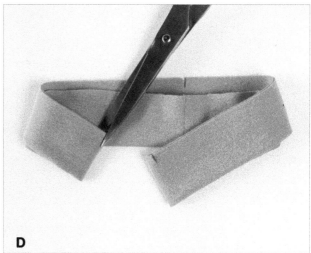

D

E

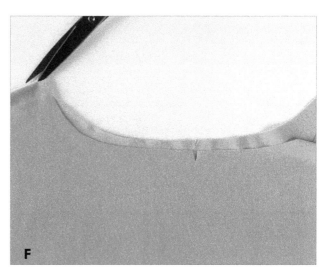

F

Applying the Binding

1. With right sides together and raw edges aligned, match the clip marks on the binding with the clip marks on neck opening, with the binding seam at the center back of the garment. Pin at each clip mark (A).

2. Starting at the center back, line up the left side of the presser foot with the outer folded edge of the binding. Move the needle position to the right the distance of the finished binding. With your right hand, hold the next quarter-marked pin and stretch the binding to match the neck opening, keeping all raw edges together. Stitch from pin to pin using your left hand to control the alignment of the binding to the neck edge (B).

3. You can either trim the seam allowance close to the stitching and leave the edges raw, or use a three-thread overlock stitch to serge the raw edges together (C).

4. Finger-press the seam allowance toward the inside of the garment, which turns and exposes the front side of the binding on the right side of the garment. Position the binding under the sewing machine presser foot so the needle is positioned just above the seamline. Then, move the needle to the left position and stitch next to the seam, catching the seam allowance on the wrong side (D).

5. Once the binding is completely sewn, place the neck opening over a tailor's ham. Apply steam to the binding and hand press the binding to help form a smooth and flat curved shape (E). Allow it to dry before removing it from the ham.

• TIP •

It's easier to apply a neck binding after the shoulders seams are sewn and before the side seams are completed.

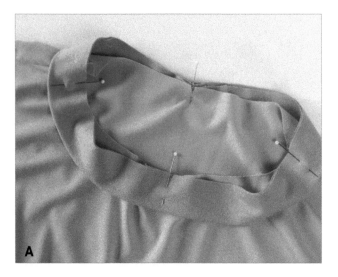

A

B

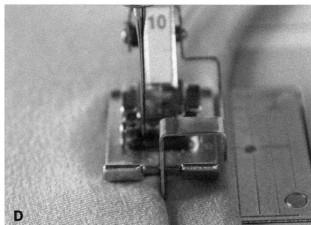

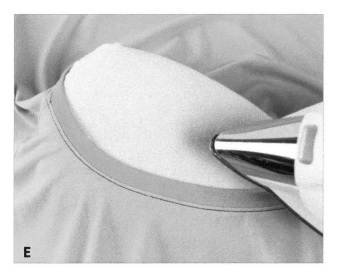

Turned and Stitched

When a binding is too thick or too sporty, a simple turn and stitched finishing method works well, especially when sewing stretch lace and other novelty textures or if you want a very smooth neck edge.

Set the differential feed so the stitches draw up the opening slightly (refer to your owner's manual). Serge the raw edge of the neck opening using a three-thread overlock stitch. Turn the serged edge to the wrong side and topstitch it in place.

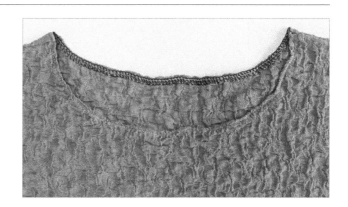

Both sides of a finished turned and stitched neck treatment.

V-neck Binding

Applying a binding to a V-shaped neckline is the same as applying any binding, the only difference is sewing the V shape.

1. Reinforce the V-shaped area of the neckline by stitching inside the seam allowance, pivoting at the V. Start and stop stitching a few inches (cm) before and after the V. Clip into the V, but not through the stitching (A).

2. It is difficult to pin the binding to the entire neckline. Starting at the center back and with right sides together, pin the binding to the neckline up to the center of the V, with the last pin in the clipped point of the V. Begin stitching at the center back and continue stitching up to the last pin at center of the V. Leave the needle in the fabric, raise the presser foot and pivot the work, allowing the clipped V to open up. The rest of the binding can now be pinned to the other side of the garment in order to complete the seam. Trim the seam allowance close to the stitching (B).

3. Without turning the binding to the inside of the garment, fold both the garment and the binding along the center front with the right sides together. Stitch only through the binding, along the centerfold (C). This helps the binding take the shape of the neckline. Clip the binding seam allowance to the V. Follow steps 4–5 in Applying the Binding on page 108 to finish the neckline.

Cowl Neck

Attaching a cowl is nothing more than sewing a wide binding to a neckline. Use the same pattern piece as for a standard binding, only make it substantially wider or any width that you desire. A cowl can be doubled like a binding or a single layer and hemmed on one edge. Either way, it is applied in the same manner as the standard binding (see page 108).

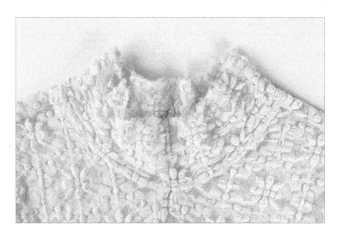

Attaching Sleeves

The stretch inherent in knit fabrics makes it easy to ease shaped sleeves into an armhole opening or to sew them flat to armhole edge before the side seams are stitched.

Flat Method

Sometimes, sleeves are attached flat (before the underarm seam is stitched) to garments that are still flat (before the side seams are stitched). This method is usually done on T-shirts and casual tops. Shoulder seams are stitched first, and then the top of the sleeve is stitched to the armhole with right sides together. In this situation, the sleeve and garment edges align evenly, so it is a matter of simply matching the notches and markings and sewing the sleeves to the garment using the seam of your choice.

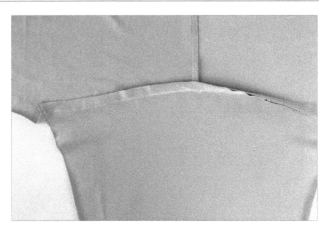

In the Round

This method is used when the sleeve cap is more curved and needs to be eased into the armhole opening. These sleeves are typically found in more fitted garments such as blouses, dresses, and jackets. The side seams and the sleeve seams are sewn first, so the insertion is literally "in the round," a tubular sleeve inserted into an armhole opening.

1. Prepare the sleeves as you would for a woven fabric. Sew a line of basting stitches just inside the seamline along the sleeve cap and between the notches; leave long thread tails at each end of the stitching. Gently pull the bobbin thread to ease the fabric and add shape to the sleeve cap. Place the sleeve over the tapered end of a tailor's ham and steam the fullness of the seam allowance, gently pressing the stitching (A).

2. With right sides together, pin the sleeve into the armhole, matching seams and other match points. Starting at the top of the sleeve, roll the seam allowance over your fingers and insert a pin perpendicular to the basting. Moving down one side of the sleeve between the top, the notches, and the underarm seam, roll sections over your fingers to ease the sleeve into the armhole opening; continue to pin regularly. When one side is done, start at the top and repeat on the other side (B).

3. Once the sleeve is pinned in place, stitch just inside the basting stitches with the sleeve side facing up. Leave the seam unfinished or serge with the three-thread stitch (C). Repeat for the other sleeve.

4. Place the sleeve over the tailor's ham or use a press mitt to lightly hand press the sleeve from the outside of the garment. Avoid pressing the sleeve flat after you have worked so hard to build shape into it.

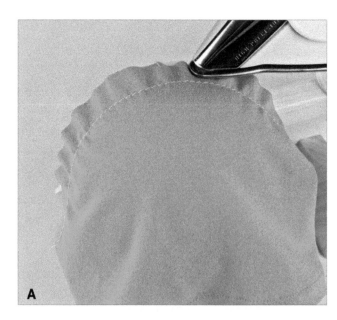

A

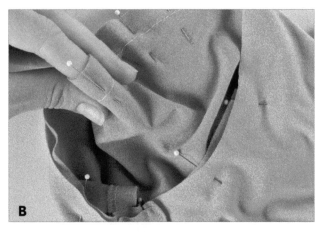

B

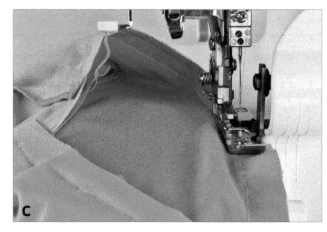

C

Elasticized Waists

Most skirts and pants with elasticized waists feature elastic in a fabric or ribbon casing or an exposed elastic inside the garment.

Types of Elastic

There are five general categories of elastic.

Braided Elastic

Braided elastic is identified by parallel ribs, that run the length of the elastic. It is available in several widths, it narrows when stretched, and snags during stitching. It is most often used inside neckline casings and sleeve hems.

Knit Elastic

Knit elastics are soft and don't narrow when stretched. You can sew through these elastics so they are typically used inside casings or exposed in pajamas, athletic wear, and pants and skirts made in light- to mid-weight fabrics.

Woven Elastic

Woven elastic, called "no-roll" elastic is strong and characterized by vertical ribs. These elastics are used in casings in mid- to heavyweight fabrics for pants and skirts.

Lingerie Elastic

Lingerie elastic features a scalloped or picot decorative edge. It is generally used on bras, undies, and lingerie, but it's fun to use in children's clothing, too.

Elastic Ribbon

Elastic ribbon looks like grosgrain ribbon with a groove down the center, which helps the ribbon fold over an edge, forming a binding. It is available in many solid colors as well as fun patterns and is used for sleek neck bindings, waistbands, and decorative edgings on sportswear, athletic wear, and childrenswear.

• Applying Elastic Ribbon •

Applying elastic ribbon is more challenging than applying other types of elastic.

1. Cut a length of elastic ribbon in the same ratio as neck binding and quarter mark it in the same fashion (see page 106). Trim the seam allowance from the garment.

2. Pin the raw edge of the garment along the indentation in the center of the elastic ribbon. Machine baste the fabric to the elastic ribbon (A).

3. Fold the elastic ribbon over the garment edge. Use small clips to hold it in place and a wide zigzag setting to stitch the elastic ribbon elastic to the garment (B).

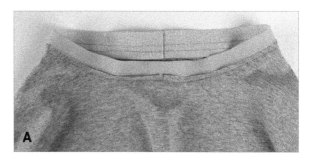

A

B

Stitching Elastic Ends

There are three ways of connecting the ends of a length of elastic to form a circle.

- Braided, knit, lingerie, and ribbon elastics can be seamed just like fabric bindings since they are so lightweight (A).
- Woven elastic needs to be overlapped and stitched (B).
- Or they should be butted and covered with a piece of fabric or ribbon (C).

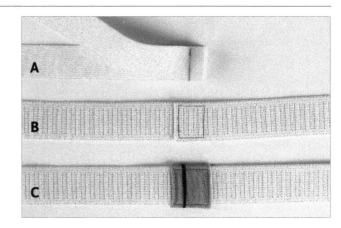

Elastic in a Casing

Creating an elastic casing in knits fabric is just as easy as in woven fabrics.

There are two types of elastic casings. One is simply the top edge of the garment pressed to the inside and the other is a separate waistband. Whichever way you wish to create the casing, simply leave an opening in the stitching that forms the casing (often in the center back) through which to insert the elastic.

Attach a bodkin or large safety pin to one end of the elastic and feed the elastic through the casing. Then use one of the methods above to secure the ends of the elastic together. Complete the stitching to close the opening in the casing.

Exposed Elastic

Many knit garments, from athletic wear to high fashion skirts and pants, feature exposed elastic as a waistline finish.

1. Measure the finished waist circumference on the pattern rather than the garment to get an accurate number. Cut the elastic to this length.

2. Sew the ends of the elastic together with ½" (1.3 cm) seam allowance; press the seam open. This makes the length of the elastic 1" (2.5 cm) smaller than the circumference of the garment.

3. Fold the elastic in half and mark the center front directly opposite the seam.

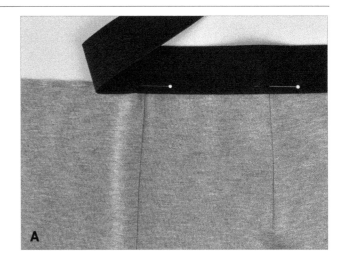

4. On the right side of the garment, chalk-mark a line ⅜" (9 mm) from the raw edge of the waistline. Pin the wrong side of the elastic to the right side of the waistline with the elastic along the chalk-marked line. Match the center back and center front (A).

5. Set your sewing machine to a 2 mm (.08 inch) long by 4 mm (.16 inch) wide zigzag stitch or a stretch stitch. Stitch the elastic to the garment, stretching the elastic slightly to fit the waistline (B).

6. Turn the elastic to the inside of the garment, forming a facing. On the right side of the garment, stitch vertically through all the layers (fabric and elastic) along all vertical seams (center front/back, side seams, darts, etc.) to secure the elastic in place (C).

Buttonholes

There are a few tricks for sewing buttonholes in knits so they lie flat without puckers and they don't stretch out.

It is important to make a lot of practice buttonholes, recording the various stitch adjustments until you make the perfect buttonhole. Always practice on the same number of layers as in the garment and in the same direction as the final buttonhole. Buttonholes tend to look better if they are sewn parallel to the rib of the knit.

How to Make a Buttonhole

1. Stabilize the area by placing one or two layers of tricot interfacing between the fabric layers (A).

2. Place lightweight paper under the work and next to the throat plate when stitching the buttonholes. Pattern tissue paper works well (B).

3. Increase the stitch length, especially when sewing lightweight knits. You do not want a really densely sewn buttonhole. If you have a preprogrammed buttonhole for sewing knits on your machine, use it. Stitch the buttonhole (C).

4. Cut the buttonhole open with a special button-hole-cutting tool. This two-piece tool consists of a cutting blade and a small block of wood. The beveled blade on the cutter avoids cutting the threads (D).

5. You can also use a seam ripper, but proceed with caution because it is easy to inadvertently cut the threads. If you do use a seam ripper, place pins at each end to act as fences to prevent you from cutting into the thread ends (E).

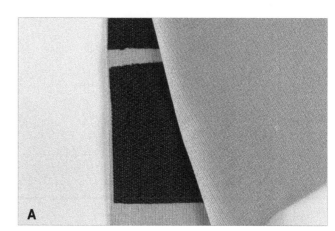

A

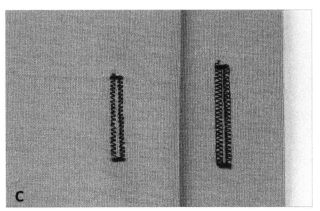

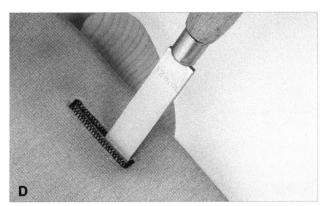

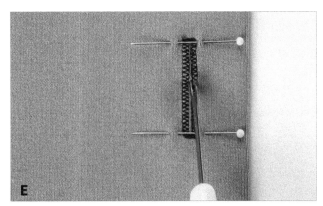

• Corded Buttonholes •

Corded buttonholes are very stable and unlikely to stretch out of shape. They are heavier-looking buttonholes and are most suited to mid- to heavyweight knits, not tissue weight knits.

1. Cut a 12" (30.5 cm) length of buttonhole twist (cording). Following your sewing machine's instructions, wrap the thread around the hook on the back of the buttonhole foot. When the machine starts stitching, the presser foot will automatically stitch over the cording to make a raised bead (A).

2. Trim off the ends of the buttonhole twist to neaten the button-hole. The cording will be completely hidden (B).

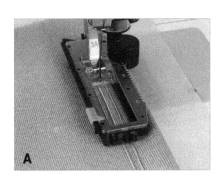

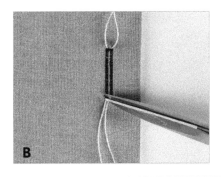

Invisible Zippers

Sometimes a zipper can be eliminated in a knit garment because of the stretch factor. But when a zipper is needed, an invisible zipper is the best option.

To install an invisible zipper, you will need a special zipper foot specifically designed for invisible zipper installations, as well as a presser foot that swings from side to side for securing the bottom of the zipper. Some machines do not come with this type of zipper foot, but you can purchase a generic sliding zipper foot that attaches to an adaptor for this purpose.

Do not sew the seam until after the zipper is installed.

1. Fuse 1" (2.5 cm)-wide strips of lightweight tricot interfacing to the wrong side of the opening, centered over the seamlines (A).

2. Chalk-mark the seam allowances on the right side of the garment and mark points ¾" (1.9 cm) from the top edge of the garment.

3. On the right side of the garment, press strips of fusible web tape within the seam allowances and remove the paper covering (B).

4. Open the zipper and lightly press the coils of the zipper open, taking care not to melt the coils.

5. Finger press one half of the zipper along one seam allowance so the zipper stop aligns with the marking near the top edge and the coils align with the marked seam allowance. Fuse the zipper tape in place.

6. Install the invisible zipper foot. Starting at the top and on the right side of the garment opening, stitch the zipper tape in place as far as possible toward the end of the zipper (C).

7. Repeat for the other side of the zipper, checking to make sure the zipper is not twisted.

8. To finish sewing the bottom of the zipper, change to the presser foot that moves from side to side.

9. Move the foot out of the way of the needle. With right sides of the fabric together, insert the needle into the previous stitches about ½" (1.3 cm) from the end of the stitching (steps 7 and 8). Use the hand wheel to walk the machine for a few stitches so that all stitches are on top of one another (D).

10. Once the stitches have bypassed the bottom of the zipper, change to a standard presser foot and finish stitching the seam (E).

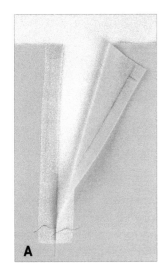

A

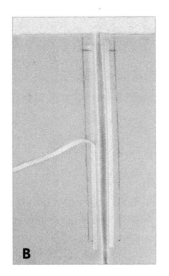

B

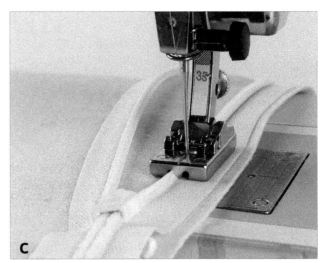

C

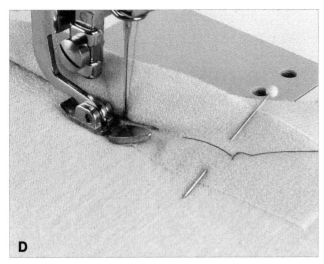

D

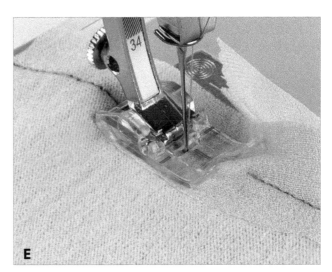

E

Ribbing

Although ribbing is used at necklines, it's more commonly used for cuffs and hem bands. When using ribbing at a neckline, use the same technique as described on page 108 for neck binding.

Making a Rib Cuff

Because ribbing stretches so much, cuffs need to be smaller than the garment opening.

1. Measure your wrist. Cut each cuff: 10% to 25% shorter (depending on the amount of stretch of the fabric) than the wrist measurement + the width of 2 seam allowances × 2 times the desired width + the width of 2 seam allowances.

2. Fold the cuff in half widthwise with the right sides together. Either sew or serge the edges together (A).

3. Fold the cuff in half lengthwise, with the raw edges aligned. Place a pin at the seam and another pin at the opposite fold. Repeat this process on the sleeve (or leg opening). Pin the cuff to the right side of the sleeve (or leg opening), matching all raw edges and pins (B).

4. Starting at one pin, begin sewing or serging, stretching the cuff between pins to match the sleeve (or leg opening). Stitch from pin to pin (C).

A

B

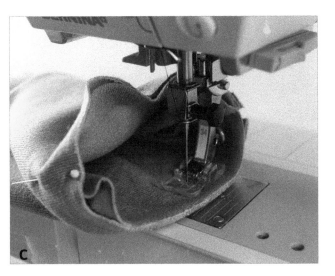

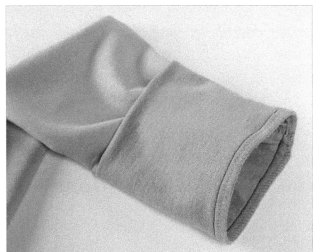

The inside of the finished cuff with a serged edge.

Garment with ribbed cuff, hem band, and neckline.

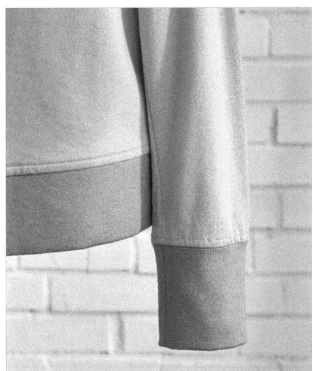

Pockets

Since knits don't ravel, it is possible to remove the seam allowances and apply a patch pocket with raw edges showing. If you prefer a more finished look, turn the seam allowances to the wrong side.

Using a Pocket Template

Use a pocket template to help control the size of the pocket and prevent distortion.

1. To make a template, trace the finished size of the pocket pattern onto a piece of cardboard or a manila file folder (A), using a tracing wheel and tracing paper. Cut out the template with a rotary cutter.

2. Use the pocket pattern to cut the pocket from the fabric. Finish the top of the pocket according to the pattern instructions.

3. Place a piece of tissue paper on an ironing surface, with the pocket, wrong side facing up, on top of the paper. Position the template in the center of the pocket. Bring the paper and the pocket seam allowances up and over the edges of the template. Press through all the layers (B). This method keeps the edges smooth and symmetrical and avoids burning your fingers.

4. To prevent pockets from shifting when stitching them to the garment, press strips of fusible web tape on the wrong side of the pocket, remove the paper covering, and fuse the pocket in place before topstitching (C).

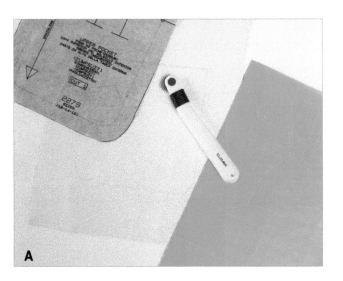

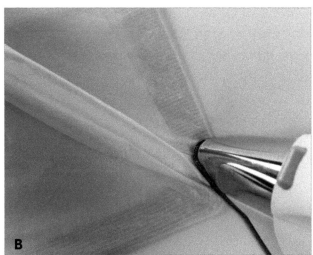

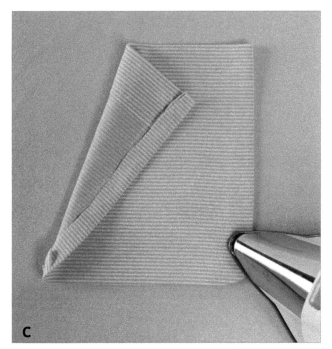

Darts

Darts are not always necessary in knit garments since the fabrics are so stretchy, but when darts are needed, it is important to sew them with care, especially in tissue and lightweight knits where there show-through is possible.

1. To sew darts accurately, chalk-mark the stitching lines of the dart. Begin stitching at the outside edge (no need to backstitch), sew along the stitching line and start to taper the stitching toward the fabric fold about ½" (1.3 cm) from the end point of the dart. End the stitching at the fold and leave thread tails (A).

2. To retain the shape formed by the dart, steam press the dart in one direction over a tailor's ham. Apply hand pressure and avoid pressing with the iron beyond the stitching (B).

A

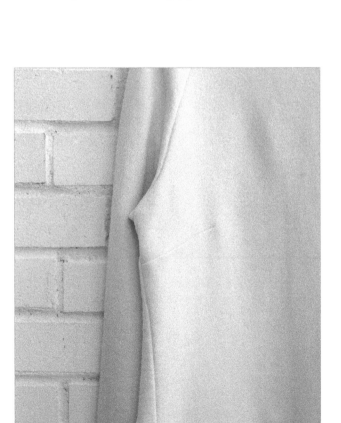

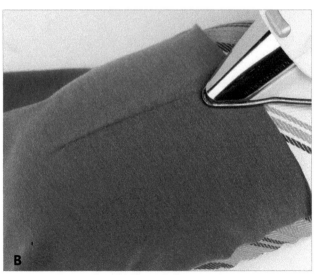

B

Darts can be more than just simple bust or hip darts for fitting the curves of a body. Sometimes they are strategic design lines that create shaping and architectural interest in non-traditional places such as darts that are left open at the ends for a softly pleated and draped effect, or long darts that begin at the hemline of a dress and continue to just below the bust, creating a bell-shape.

Embellishments

Hand stitching adds a hand-crafted look to a garment. Use three or four strands of cotton embroidery floss to appliqué an interesting motif along a raw-edge hemline. Use a simple running stitch, a blanket stitch or a traditional appliqué stitch to outline the edge of a complementary color of knit or mimic the motif in another place such as a sleeve edge.

Linings

The idea of lining a knit garment is somewhat counterintuitive, and most knit garments can stand on their own without underlinings and linings, but there are some garments in which a lining is a nice addition. Lining adds structure, conceals the inner construction of a garment, and adds longevity to a fine garment. Tailored dresses, slim-fitting skirts, and elegant jackets, often constructed in stable knits, benefit from the addition of a lining.

If you have selected a knit fabric for its color, texture, or overall character and stretch is not a factor in the fit and appearance, then use a traditional woven lining such as Bemberg rayon, silk crepe de Chine, or silk charmeuse. When lining is needed for some support or to make a sheer fabric more opaque, choose a lining that has stretch such as tricot. You can also use a woven lining as long as it is cut on the bias so it stretches enough to work with the knit fabric.

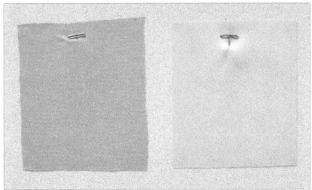

6

Activewear and Lingerie

Making clothes for an active lifestyle has gotten much easier with all the wonderful four-way stretch fabrics available to the home sewer, and a few key sewing techniques. Sewing lingerie is just as easy and rewarding.

Activewear

Swimsuits, yoga pants and tops, leotards, leggings, and even tights are easy to find in the stores, but finding the right shape and size to fit is another issue. Making your own can be fun and fast, especially when you use the right materials and techniques.

Fabrics

Activewear fabrics are characterized by their super stretch and recovery properties thanks to the addition of spandex. Many of them are moisture wicking. There is a tremendous range of these fabrics, most made from synthetic fibers such as polyester and nylon, with some percentage of spandex fibers to ensure the four-way stretch. Consider using waffle textured knits, specialty knits called SeaCell, which are made from seaweed cellulose and are cool to the touch, various sheer weights of power mesh, and any of the fabulous activewear fabrics in exciting colors, patterns, and textures.

Some activewear garments, particularly swimwear, should be lined for modesty and comfort. The most common swimsuit lining is made of nylon, but you will find polyester/cotton/nylon blends, too. Most are a nude color and are generally sold alongside the swimsuit fabrics.

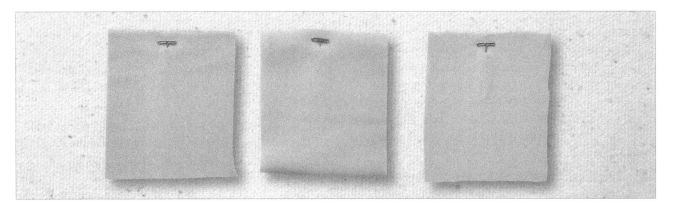

Layout and Cutting

Place the pattern pieces on the fabric so the most stretch going around your body. Use sharp pins and pin within the seam allowances because these fabrics snag easily. You can cut with scissors, but using a rotary cutter keeps the cut line smooth and accurate.

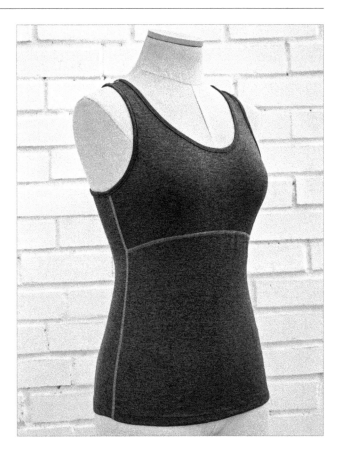

Sewing Tips

While sewing these four-way stretch fabrics can be tricky, there are several things you can do to make the process easier.

- Just as when sewing on any other knit fabric, use polyester thread or wooly nylon thread for a softer feel. Experiment with both needle and thread choices. You can try universal, ballpoint, or stretch needles. If skipped stitches are a problem, change the thread brand and the type and size of the needle until you find the right combination for smooth and even stitches.

- While these super stretch fabrics can be sewn on a sewing machine, they are best sewn on a serger to keep the seams as flat as possible so the seam allowances don't rub against your skin as you work out. A four-thread serged seam (A) is the best stitch choice for swimsuit weight fabric and it holds up well over time and use.

- The flatlocked serged seam (B) is the flattest seam. It is a good choice for scuba-weight fabric. Refer to page 89 for complete instructions.

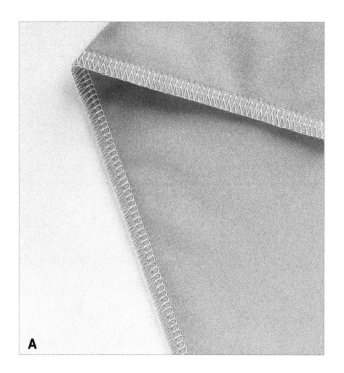

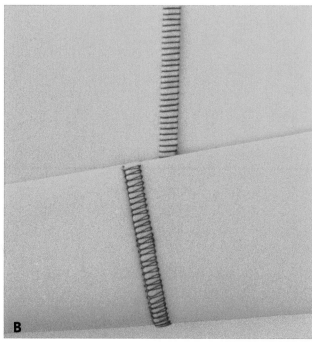

- To sew seams on a sewing machine, set the machine to a narrow zigzag stitch with a stitch width of .5 and stitch length of 2.5. Trim the seam allowance to ¼" (6 mm) wide (C) and then finger-press the seam allowance to one side. Topstitch on the right side with a 4 mm (.16 inch)-wide zigzag stitch through all layers (D). Make sure the zigzag stitch covers the raw edges on the inside of the garment.

- Rather than sewing a standard seam, overlap the raw edges and zigzag stitch (E).

- The most important hem feature on activewear garments is adequate stretch without popped stitches. Coverstitch and twin-needles hems are the best choices because they are simple and flat. A large zigzag stitch works well on heavier fabrics (F).

C

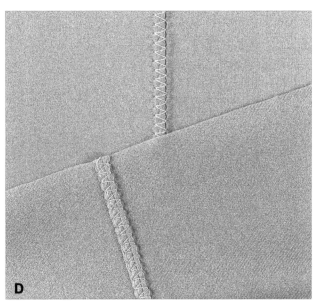

D

E

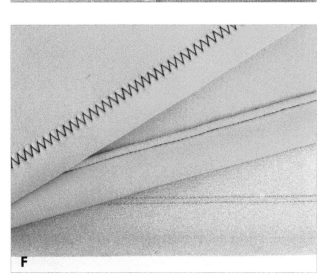

F

Elastic Finishes

The best elastic to use for activewear and especially swimwear is an elastic that has neoprene (a synthetic rubber) in it so that it is resistant to salt and chlorine. These elastics are available in white, black, and natural. Clear elastic is another option.

Your pattern may include a guide for how long to cut the elastic. If not, refer to page 106 for how to calculate length using the ⅝ ratio.

For necklines: Overlap the ends of the elastic and sew them together. Divide the neckline and the elastic into fourths and match these points when sewing the elastic to the fabric. See page 115 for instructions.

For leg openings: Apply the elastic in a 1 to 1 ratio in the front of the leg and stretch it to fit the back leg, so the garment cups more below the derriere.

1. Cut the seam allowance to the exact width of the elastic you are using. Pin the elastic to the wrong side of the fabric, aligning the edge of the elastic to the raw edge of the fabric. Use a wide zigzag or a four-thread serger stitch to attach it to the edge (A).

2. Turn the width of the elastic to the wrong side of the garment and topstitch it in place, using a twin needle or coverstitch for maximum stretch (B).

For waistlines: see page 113.

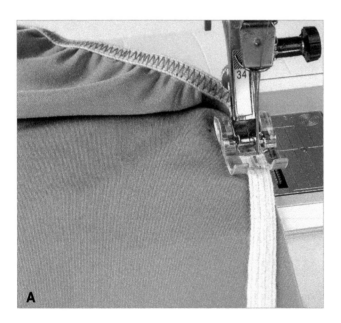

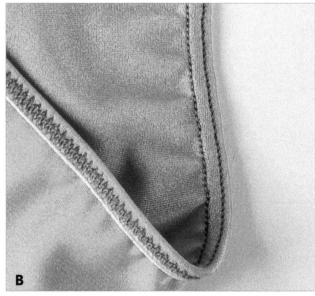

Lingerie

Beautiful woven fabrics such as silk charmeuse and crepe de chine are commonly used for sewing slips, panties, and camisoles, but knitted fabrics such as tricot, power mesh, stretch lace, and other open weave fabrics are just as popular.

Types of Lingerie Elastics

The most uniquely different aspect of sewing lingerie fabrics is the selection and application of elastics. The overall appearance of lingerie is enhanced with the addition of elastics, as both utilitarian and decorative trims.

Decorative edge elastics feature a scalloped edge or a picot edge that is visible beyond the finished fabric edge. Stretch lace elastic, with or without seam allowances, can be applied on top of the fabric, nestled in a seam, or as a peek-a-boo insertion anywhere within the garment. All these elastics are available in many colors.

Applying Decorative-Edge Elastic

1. So the decorative edge shows, pin the elastic on top of the right side of the garment, aligning the straight edge of the elastic with the raw edge of the fabric. Use a narrow zigzag stitch to stitch near the decorative edge (A).

2. To finish, fold the elastic to the wrong side and use a stretch zigzag stitch close to the straight edge of the elastic (B).

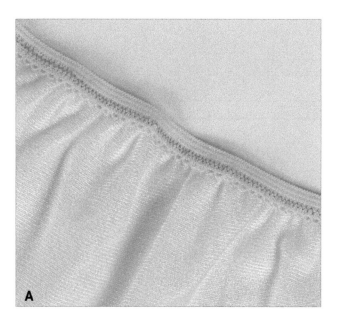

A

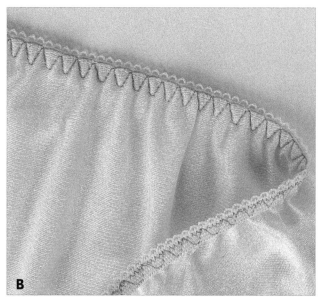

B

Applying Stretch Lace

Stretch lace with a seam allowance is applied in the same manner as decorative-edge elastic by simply allowing the amount of lace you want to be exposed (A).

To apply stretch lace with two decorative edges to the raw edges of the fabric, pin the wrong side of the lace to the right side of the fabric so that the outer edge of the lace is even with the raw edge of the garment. Use a medium zigzag stitch to sew along the inner edge of the lace. Use small scissors to trim the fabric under the lace away close to the zigzag stitches (B).

To create a peek-a-boo lace trim effect, place the wrong side of the lace on the right side of the fabric. This can be done anywhere in the garment, it doesn't need to applied to a garment edge. Zigzag stitch both edges of the lace to the fabric. Use small scissors to trim away the fabric between the two rows of stitches, behind the lace (C).

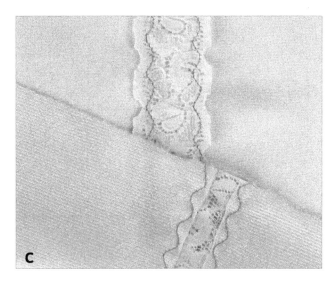

Resources

Cloth House
ww.clothhouse.com
Fabrics

Elliott Berman Textiles
www.elliottbermantextiles.com
Knitwear fabrics

Jalie Patterns
www.jalie.com
Knitwear patterns

Christine Jonson Patterns
www.cjpatterns.com
Knitwear patterns

Lingerie Secrets by Jan Bones
www.sewinglingerie.com
Lingerie Patterns

Mokuba NY
www.mokubany.com
Elastic ribbons

Mood Fabrics
www.moodfabrics.com
Knitwear fabric

Nancy's Notions
www.nancysnotions.com
Sewing notions

Pamela's Patterns
www.pamelaspatterns.com
Knitwear patterns

Seattle Fabrics
www.seattlefabrics.com
Athletic wear fabrics

Sew Sassy Fabrics
www.sewsassy.com
Lingerie fabrics

Style Arc Patterns
www.stylearc.com
Knitwear patterns

The Ribbonerie
www.ribbonerie.com
Elastic ribbons

The Sewing Workshop
www.sewingworkshop.com
Patterns, knitwear fabrics, notions

Wawak Sewing Supplies
www.wawak.com
Sewing notions

Zoelee's Fabrics & Sewing School
www.zoelees.com
Swimwear fabrics, tricot, elastics

Patterns Featured

The following patterns from The Sewing Workshop are featured in this book as noted below. For more information on these and other patterns, visit www.sewingworkshop.com.

Acknowledgments

Thanks to my junior high, high school, and college sewing teachers, I had the benefit of being taught by the best of trained educators. Real inspiration and contemporary methods of construction came later thanks to many of the teachers at The Sewing Workshop school in San Francisco, which I owned for twelve years. The editors of *Threads* magazine and Trisha Malcolm of Sixth & Spring Books gave me the freedom to hone my skills as a writer, which of course required research and samples and hours at the sewing machine. Dort Johnson, my local mentor and who helped me open my first fabric store, taught me not only about sewing, but how to teach and inspire students to want to make fashionable clothes. My mother let me use her sewing machine before I could even use the scissors, and my daughter keeps me current as she moves forward in the sewing and fashion world and looks fabulous every day.

About the Author

Linda Lee's training and experience as an interior designer has come in handy as she travels the country teaching the art of combining beautiful fabrics for the fashion-conscious home sewer. Along with teaching fitting skills and fine sewing techniques, she is known for designing patterns under the name of The Sewing Workshop, a line of patterns for the modern sewer who is interested in architecturally interesting styles to flatter with flare.

Along with four talented staff members, she operates out of her pattern-making studio in Topeka, Kansas, where she conducts sewing retreats and you will find a huge inventory of fabrics that are sold online. She produces a monthly series of inspirational tutorials called Sew Confident! in which she breaks down the latest fashion trends into real-life sewing experiences for people who want to sew better than they can buy.

With eleven Craftsy classes and thirteen books under her belt, Linda has the depth of experience and enthusiasm needed to pass on the fine art of sewing clothes to her students.

Linda loves cats, fashion labels Marni and Akris, Roger Federer, vintage hand stitching, Fillmore Street in San Francisco, and Oreo Blizzards.

Index